You Can't
Ride a Yak

LOOKING FOR YAKS AND FINDING GOD'S CALL IN NEPAL

SARAH REARDON

Ark House Press
arkhousepress.com

Cataloguing in Publication Data:
Title: *You Can't Ride A Yak: Looking for yaks and finding God's call in Nepal*
ISBN: 978-0-6451031-3-7 (pbk)
Subjects: Biography; Mission; Christian Living;
Other Authors/Contributors: Reardon, Sarah

Cover image: © Neville Walter
In-text illustrations: © Neville Walter
Cover design and layout by initiateagency.com

Dedicated to my husband Danny, who always believed more than I, that this was all possible. He makes me look better than I actually am. He took me to Nepal, fulfilling some unseen, but divine plan. For your forgiveness and grace – thank you!

Hopefully one day you will ride a yak.

Acknowledgements

Thanks to my editor, Rachel Higgins
for her accurate eye, and heart.

Thanks to my children, their spouses, and my grandchildren:
you put up with my obsessions and have fun with me.
Thanks to Jacob for coming to Nepal twice, and to
Jessica for having the heart and mouth of a prophet.

Thanks to my friends who have supported my crazy ideas,
prayed and often followed me into action: Kim, Tim and
Carole, Joel and Liz, Carla, Sabina, Jill and Peter, Esther,
Debbie and Pierre, Paula, Tony and Kez, Cathy, Ashok and
Romila, Saimon, Keshav and Pramisa, Parasu and Shon.

Thanks to Uncle David and Aunty Pam for showing
me how to live for Christ and passing on the baton.

From everyone who has been given much, much will be demanded; and from the one who has been entrusted with much, much more will be asked.

(Luke 12:48b)

Prologue

Struggling for breath, I slung my daypack over my shoulder. *How will we be able to do this for two weeks?* I thought as I tried to keep pace with my husband, Danny, who was carrying our extra-large duffel bags.

As we disembarked from the small Twin Otter aircraft, the moist chill in the air was a surprise after experiencing the warmer, dry air of Kathmandu. We were at 2860 metres above sea level. The pathway ascending out of Lukla Airport snaked around the tarmac towards the main village. As we made our way up the gentle slope, my lungs didn't seem able to find the air needed to breathe. We wondered where the guide was. Our flight had departed from Kathmandu two hours late due to cloud and fog. This caused our arrival into Lukla, the gateway to the Everest trekking region, to be much later than planned. We thought our welcome party must have already given up on waiting for us because of the delay. So, without any other ideas, we decided to make our own way towards the village. As we made our way out of the airport, numerous Nepali men bombarded us with questions.

"You have guide?"

"You need porter?"

"Who you meeting?"

"Who you trek with?"

It was all new for us, and we rushed to grab our bags from the trolley before some of those 'helpful' young men took them off our hands and wandered away with our precious trekking gear. Had our decision one week earlier been crazy? When we paid the trekking company for two staff and booked a flight to one of the world's most dangerous airports. Now here we were, looking for a Nepali guide named Saimon, while carrying a large yellow envelope containing thousands of rupees.

Finally, we managed to push our way through the throng of other eager trekkers; porters gathering boxes of noodles and beer, and dozens of hands reaching to snatch bags. Free from the frenzy, we rushed up the short path into Lukla. A few men had told us they thought someone called Saimon was at the Khumbu Lodge, so following their hand gestures, we set off in that general direction. That's when we realised that there was less air, and the puffing began.

"You Australian, sir? Madam, you Australian?" Someone suddenly asked from behind us.

"We are right mate, we don't need help, we are ok," Danny puffed out.

"No, you Australian? You need guide?" He tried to take the bags from Danny's hand.

We ignored him and kept walking, afraid of being taken advantage of.

"Please, you are Danny, sir? I take your bags."

Stopping to look around, we met a slight framed, intent Nepali man with deep brown eyes, wearing a cap, joggers, dress trousers, and a button-up shirt. With a flash of white teeth, he smiled at us and said, "I am Saimon."

Minutes later, we entered a warm dining room in the lodge, ordered tea and eggs and sat down; already overwhelmed at all the new sights and sensations. After the initial introductions, we handed Saimon the yellow envelope and enquired about the porter. He looked in the envelope and promptly went to pick up our bags as if to test their weight.

"Your bags not heavy, I carry them for you and be your guide. I do work of porter and guide and you pay me for both. What you think?" He said as he returned to our table.

I remember then that a 'rip off' radar and an 'I don't know if I trust you' feeling crept in. I made 'oh no' faces to Danny, who quickly asked if we could talk privately about this. When Saimon returned, we laid out the deal.

"If you do the work of both, then fine. But don't complain if it gets too hard. You said you could do it."

I think they shook hands. After some more tea, and probably buying some Snickers bars, the three of us started out towards our first night's destination. A village three and a half hours away called Phak Ding.

My intention was that I would complete the 14-day trek to and from Gokyo Lakes, then return to Australia and continue on with life as it had been before.

I had no idea what journey I was really about to begin.

Chapter 1

Just Go

I had lived in Queensland, Australia, all my life; except for a brief stint in the USA as an exchange student when I was 17. In April 2012, at the end of our Cairns wet season, Danny came home and announced that he would be going on a trek in Nepal with a female friend of ours. This announcement came after many years of him talking about his great memories of a 12-month overland journey from Indonesia to London that his parents had taken him on. During that year, they spent some time in Nepal. The stories of trekking in Nepal, the coloured fabrics, friendly people, and ancient buildings had been retold on various occasions over our years of marriage. So, while I was busy working, parenting, socialising, and doing all the things that other Australian families were doing, Danny had been thinking about other things. He had been thinking about that little country stuck between China and India; sitting beneath the world's highest mountain range—the Himalayas. He had now decided that, after raising his family, it was time to pursue the adventure again and revisit this colourful place.

I was not interested. My response was, "Oh, you are going to Nepal with …, are you?"

When he confirmed that anyone was welcome, and it was just that she indicated that she wanted to go.

I replied, "I'm still not going."

In my mind, Nepal was full of challenging hiking trails that demanded unimaginable fitness and dedication. It was far away from anything I had seen or known. Over the years, I had glanced at the photos from Danny's visit back in 1982. Photos of monkeys, prayer flags flapping in the wind, snow on the ground, and wrinkled brown faces in unusual clothing. Stories told of tiny carved wooden shop fronts, overflowing with bits and pieces of interesting and quirky objects like locks, religious statues, singing bowls and incense sticks. And the sacred River Ganges that flowed all the way from India, where the dead were given their last respects before ending their journey as ash floating toward their afterlife. All these new and foreign things competed for space in my mind, as I tried to make the decision. But it was the idea of an arduous trek that really disinterested me the most. What could I possibly want to go there for?

A few days later, I recounted this conversation to our eldest daughter, Jessica. She often has the knack of, what I would call 'prophetic insight,' and promptly said, "Mum, Dad always does everything you want…Just go!"

For some reason unknown to me at the time, I felt a distinct shift in my attitude. A desire began growing within me, to go with Danny to visit this strange, foreign, and mystical place called Nepal.

So, I once again dug out the old blue photo album from 1982. There behind the yellowing adhesive film, captured in fading Kodak prints, were the brown wrinkly faces. I looked at the characters in the pictures. Two men who must have been porters, carried bags by a rope that bore the weight on their foreheads. They wore rubber slip-on sandals and happy, toothy smiles. On the trails, the snow sat in clumps, melting as April turned winter to spring. In the images of Kathmandu, the capital city, was the sacred river. Brown and important, flowing between countries as it guided death to the afterlife. I stared, gazing through a window to Danny's memories. It was as if those pictures captured me here in Cairns, 30 years later. We began to train and make plans.

Nepal was to be part of a three-month, long service leave trip that would include: Thailand, India, a month long house exchange with a German family, and another month in Paris. It was going to be our first time doing something like this without our three children, and my first time travelling in Asia. There was a lot to organise—visas, vaccines, trekking gear, flights, and arranging things that needed doing at home while we would be away. But the most challenging part of the preparation was for the trek. One of the great things about going to Nepal is that anyone who has already been there, takes great delight in sharing everything they learned. In fact, tourists who have been to Nepal are possibly the biggest advertisers for the country. They are a wealth of knowledge about trekking, food, safety, weather, and the training required. They delight in telling you about getting diarrhea from drinking the water, staying at cheap and quirky hostels, altitude sickness, friendly shopkeepers, and freezing nights at high altitude. I began to take note of everything they had to say.

Fortunately for me, we had a friend, Kerry, who had experience trekking in Nepal, and many other outdoor exploration adventures. So, along with her husband, Tony, they happily took us under their wing and began to help Danny train me to hike. Danny and I bought boots, following the advice to wear them in, and hiked our local mountain trails around the Whitfield Range and beyond. Our first walk with Kerry and Tony was meant to be an introductory one. My hiking experience amounted to several hours in National Parks when I was younger and very short walks near my home. I had never done a multi-day hike, and especially not one that involved the possibility of snow and acute mountain sickness. So, the first hike up to Lake Morris, a round trip of about 2.5 hours seemed like a good start.

Twenty minutes in, I felt faint. We hadn't stopped climbing during that whole time, and I needed to source energy from somewhere. Kerry happily chatted to me while I merely struggled to breathe. I since learnt that her nickname is 'the Gazelle.' My legs were beginning to burn, and my heart rate was probably over 170. I recognised that I had some work to do. It appears there are ways to walk, and 'there are ways to walk.'

"Push off with your down leg."

"Breathe before you get to the steps."

"Brace your core when you step down."

However, everyone was encouraging. It wasn't more than a few months later that I was hiking up hills for 4 hours at a time and pushing myself in cross-fit classes. My body began to respond.

I remember one day straining to keep up with Danny on the Blue Arrow trail, the 2 hours of humid uphill draining my energy.

Danny's encouragement was always, "If you go hard here, you can relax when you get to Nepal. If you prepare now, it will be easier when you get there".

So, I continued hiking my way up and down hours of trails, carrying weights in my backpack, and reading websites about mountain sickness.

Then November came. It was time to gather our gloves, thermals, water bottles, boots, gastro stop medication, Lonely Planet guide book, passports, then kiss our children and Australia goodbye. On our way through Thailand, we had our passports stamped at the Nepali Consulate. With a one-month tourist entry visa into Nepal, we landed in a Thai Airways plane at Tribhuvan International Airport, Kathmandu.

Facing the crowds of foreign faces and taxi drivers clamouring for our fares, we picked a driver. We were on our way towards the guesthouse we had chosen from Trip Advisor—The Dolphin Guesthouse. I looked through the taxi window at half-crumbled buildings and debris piled up on the sides of the road. Rubble seemed to be everywhere. Somewhere between the airport and our accommodation, I asked Danny if we were in a war zone. Thoughts of Syria kept filling my mind.

Meanwhile, women in red and green fabrics draped over their shoulders picked their way through the scooters, taxis, and cows on the roads as we ground our way through the traffic. Finishing up in a narrow laneway, we met the guesthouse owner, Mr Joshi. A cool, clean entrance and reception area welcomed us. As we climbed the four sets of marble stairs to our room, the horns and dust of the streets seemed far away. Puffing our way up each step, I wondered how we were ever going to make it through the trek we had planned, if we were struggling to climb a few stairs. The door of our room opened, and there was our new home-base for the next few weeks. Neat and compact, with a bathroom as big as a small wardrobe, and a window view of a busy courtyard below. We laughed at the simplicity of the room. Especially the way that the toilet sat directly underneath the shower rose, then promptly went outside to explore.

Walking through the streets of the tourist area, Thamel, quickly opened our eyes to the booming trekking industry in Nepal. Hundreds of other foreigners wandered the tight busy streets filled with incense, tea shops, trekking and climbing gear, and busy restaurants and cafes. We found a shop selling woollen shawls or yak wool as advertised. I looked through many of the colours, finally settling on a blue and aqua coloured one, and tried my hand at bargaining. I failed. But ended up with a shawl that I loved and met my first Nepali woman, funnily her name was also Sarah.

We spent part of the first week organising our trek and exploring the new city while enjoying eating both local and international foods. It was during that week that we met a taxi driver who introduced himself as Lama.

Lama sat in his taxi at the end of our laneway every morning. He waited on passers-by or hotel guests to hail him for business. His beaten up, Suzuki with holes in the floor and seats that caved as you sat down carried us through many boggy, bouncy, and jammed roads. We quickly learnt that *jam*, was everywhere. Every day, a traffic *jam* happened almost everywhere we went. Lama was very good at navigating jams. We enjoyed laughing with him as he made U-turns in impossible situations while maintaining the road rules.

Apparently!

It was in Lama's home that we experienced our first Nepali family hospitality. It was also the first time we became acutely aware of the existence of the caste system in Nepal. A person's caste can limit their ability to work in certain careers, or establish a business that is not acceptable for their 'status' in society. The caste system was outlawed in Nepal in 1962. Yet, in reality, it is still a challenge in many situations and contexts across the land. Sometimes it is only subtle, such as negative facial expression showing disapproval. But it can also be obvious and more detrimental. Some individuals have been shunned from their families for marrying below their caste status or chastised for befriending someone. With our western stomachs, and inexperience, when we told one of our Nepali acquaintances that we were going to dine with Lama, they rightly reminded us to take care of eating food outside the restaurants and cafes that typically catered for foreigners. But it was at the next point which we felt uncomfortable. With a serious face, he also asked us if we realised that Lama was poor. He went on to say that the food may not be what we are accustomed to eating. We thanked him for his concerns and promptly prayed before we made our way to Lama's home for a meal.

If you have never been to a Nepali home for a meal, let me tell you what will be on the menu: Dahl (lentils) and rice. There will possibly be other additions such as pickles and some meat; if it can be afforded. But the staple, and the bulk of the meal, will be lentils and rice. This meal supplies the entire nation of Nepal with their twice-daily fill of calories and energy. It quickly became our go-to. It is spicey, filling, warm, satisfying, and there is always more. Lama's wife, Gita, filled our plates; then filled them again. We were even treated to curried chicken. An honour, considering the expense it would have incurred. Though I do remember Danny checking to see that the chicken was well cooked.

Of course, it was!

We walked home happy, with a great sense of gratitude for our new friends, and the privilege of being guests in their home. We were amazed at the generosity of them having shared so much of the little that they had with us. It felt special. More than if they had a large house full of furniture, stuff, and staff. More than if they had their next month's rent already in the bank and enough to pay the school for next term's tuition. They gave what they could.

I do confess that I drank a bottle of Coke on the way home, just in case that helped to kill off any bugs that we may have picked up. We were newcomers to Nepal and had so much to learn. It was all new. But I do not remember ever feeling overwhelmed or unhappy to be there. I loved it from the first hour.

That night, in our little room at the Dolphin Guest House, we talked about the poor, and about our plenty. I prayed with newfound gratitude and awareness of the great privilege our lives had experienced. I marvelled at the challenges of the Nepali people. I wondered what it meant for me. Then I slept to the distant sounds of horns and barking dogs; awaking to the gentle cooing of pigeons on the windowsill.

It was now time to trek.

Chapter 2

Yaks and Mules

B ells.

Bells and soft Nepali singing, the smell of manure as mules and dzo (pronounced jok-ee-ohs) pass you, a whistling herder as he reminds the animal to keep to the path.

"Remember to always stay on the inside of the path when the animals come." Saimon, our guide, regularly reminded us.

Mules and dzos can get quite bossy as herds of ten, or more, of them make their way up the steep uneven paths. Their bells jingled around their necks; the cargo on their backs swung from side to side with each step —gas canisters, rice, and trekking supplies. It is best to stand up against the hillside to let them pass, or you may find yourself nudged by the animals and falling off the side of the path. Or worse, over the steep cliffs. They also have a habit regularly of letting off gas. An unpleasant experience if you are standing right behind, on a step or two below.

All these sights, sounds, and more filled the space between each step as we hiked to Gokyo Lake. This trek passes through lower altitude villages. Following the curves of the Dude Khosi (Milk River) until the lush vegetation gives way to dusty paths, tufts of dry alpine juniper, and towering giants of snowcapped peaks. Here, the thar (mountain goat) stands bold on the rocks, defiant and camouflaged, staring into the valleys while the mountain pigeon forage for something tasty in brown grasses. They are silent as we steadily climb further towards distant tea houses and small stone fences that keep yaks in during the winter.

We quickly learnt that Saimon was probably much more attentive than most of the other guides that we had observed. He carried our bags; arranged our overnight accommodation at each village; ordered our meals; helped us tie shoelaces, and unscrewed water bottle lids when we were too tired to get it right. He even washed our clothes and underwear! He was also good company. He and Danny were often heard laughing behind me as I wandered ahead leaving them to their jokes. They covered new topics every day, from the cost of cars in Australia to why the yak is never ridden like other animals.

"How come I never see anyone riding the yaks?" asked Danny.

"Oh, noooo, no, you cannot ride a yak," Saimon laughed, rolling his head from side to side.

"But why not? He is big and very strong, and can carry more than the porters every day," argued Danny.

Still, Saimon laughed.

Danny never accepted that it couldn't be done. That is how he approached most things.

There were also Saimon's attempts to teach us basic Nepali greetings, which progressed very slowly. Having never heard the language before, meant that a simple phrase took hours of practice to master.

"Tapaailaai kasto chha? How are you?"

I have to admit, Danny is great at remembering details, and he actually got the Nepali correct before I did. Not only was Saimon a patient teacher, but he was also careful with our health and diet. Although he tried to discourage us from drinking cold Coke when we were trying to acclimatise, we did not understand the reasons. To his dismay, we gulped down quite a few bottles on that trail. Years later, we learnt that it is actually better to drink warm or hot drinks when adjusting to the cold, and altitude, as it works with your body's attempts to keep your core temperature. But we were from tropical northern Australia and were used to trying to cool down. There was a lot we needed to learn.

Many Nepali people are excellent card players. Another fun fact we learnt from porters and guides we met in the dining rooms of the tea houses. One particularly memorable night we spent playing one of the local games and lost miserably. I decided to teach them our game called 'Spoons.' This game requires fast hand-eye coordination. It also involves grabbing one of the limited number of spoons from the middle of the table before anyone else gets them. Because we had practised it many times before, the young porter boys were losing each game. But it didn't take long for them to catch up and soon they were grabbing spoons too and rolling off benches in hilarious laughter.

During the days, we walked on. Sometimes down, but mostly up. It was stark, but beautiful, chilling and invigorating at the same time. My wonder at the creative powers of God made me cry many times as I stopped to breathe and take in the views. I smelt the dried flowers, and told God how beautiful it was. Danny filmed and snapped photos. We heard, "*la la, hunchha, la*," repeatedly as Saimon talked to his wife on the mobile phone. We decided that the phone network in Nepal must be very good if you could even find a connection on the isolated route to Everest.

After 7 days, despite all our efforts to acclimatise and take our time, I began to feel the effect of the altitude. We reached a tiny guest house in Luza, set in a small pocket of land at 4390m. We are the only guests, as it was the end of the trekking season, and winter was descending upon the mountains. As darkness crept into the dining room, we begged for the host to put more yak manure in the small stove in the centre of the room. Thick fog swirled around the yak farms, and the outline of Cholatse, Lobuche and other peaks that dominate the view.

As the night set in, so did a migraine and nausea. I felt the effects of fear and isolation pressing in on me. The knowledge of the remoteness and lack of medical support began to eat into my confidence. As I struggled to get warm, I began to cry. Wrapped up in my sleeping bag, sitting on the window seat with Danny and Saimon attending me, my imagination started working overtime. I wondered how this would end.

One of our neighbours back in Cairns had died of acute altitude sickness years before as she attempted to trek to Everest Base Camp. Although I was about 1200m below that height, I was feeling the effects acutely. Fear is a powerful thing. Fear and inexperience will halt you in the same situation, that years later, you will be able to overcome. But right there, at that moment, I was not well. The owner of the lodge and his wife checked in on me regularly. In hushed Nepali voices, they discussed what to do. Saimon touched my forehead and cheek as tears continuously rolled down, "Why you cry? Don't worry."

But I couldn't stop.

I asked Danny to pray for me, to seek God's presence to calm my fears and bring my body into adjustment with the situation. My migraine and nausea continued as the cold ate into my bones. At some point, the owner's wife came to me, holding a tray of hot coals she waved the smoke over me and told me to breathe it in. At first, I reacted with fear and mistrust, as my instincts told me it was some strange religious practice. But as I looked around me and at her face and listened to the words of care and kindness, I realised something new. They loved me. This was an act of love, not religion. I was overwhelmed. What goodness in a small tea house at 4390metres altitude, a dirt floor, yak manure to heat, and…I was loved.

The Neurofen and Diamox (altitude sickness medication) began to kick in for my migraine, and the best hot veg noodle soup warmed my insides. The loving care of our Nepali companions transformed my fearful night into a restful deep sleep; I awoke in calm comfort. Even though we had tried to keep the room warm, my water bottle that had sat next to me during the night was frozen solid. I think Danny had even paid extra so that the yak manure kept burning all night. I can't imagine how cold it was outside.

I cried again as we turned around in the sunshine: just 6 hours walking distance short of Gokyo Lakes. I had so wanted to make it. I so wanted Danny to make it too. But in usual Danny form, he said he was happy. He said that he was glad that I was well.

"How could I go home and tell your parents that something terrible had happened to you if we continued higher?" He asked.

Instead of heading further up the valley, we headed down. Saimon strolled behind us, perhaps feeling the disappointment of not quite making the goal. We were all a bit quiet for a few hours.

Three days later we arrived back at Lukla. The place we had started. I was well again, and we enjoyed the variety of food and accommodation that a more populated village provided. All this was nice, but meeting Saimon's sister was really special.

We were introduced to her as Didi. At the time, we did not know that 'didi' means older sister in Nepali. We simply thought it was her name. Inside her tiny, dark, smoky tea room, we met her whole family. Saimon cooked us tasty buff curry, and we drank ruksi (millet alcohol) and sweetened black coffee. It was a feast.

That night we gave Saimon our tips, a normal part of trekking culture, and thanked him for his kindness and care over the past 12 days. We promised to return in two years to trek again and walk with the yaks, smell the juniper and stare at Thamserku peak from Namche Bazar through our guesthouse window. We prayed for Saimon that his dream of owning his own restaurant and guesthouse would come to fruition and that he would be blessed as he had blessed us on our journey.

Early the next morning, the last-minute rush to board the Yeti Airline plane arrived. We taxied along the tiny airstrip and launched off into the space between the mountain peaks and the river valleys below. *See you in two years,* we thought.

But two years was too long.

Chapter 3

What I have, I give to you

I remember exactly where we were when I said, "I want to go back to Nepal in October this year." We had just arrived home to Australia in January, after three months of travelling. By February, my thoughts wormed their way out of my mouth. We were on our way into town, driving past the local touch football grounds when I said it. I said what I had thought about constantly for weeks. And so, we did.

Instead of waiting two years, as we originally planned, we returned in less than one year. The goal was to conquer the trek we had not completed last time. This time we decided we would take longer to acclimatise, so planned a three-week trek called The Classic. Instead of the flight into Lukla, we would bus to Jiri, then walk the extra week to Lukla, hoping that we would better adjust to the altitude. I encouraged myself with the thought that this was the same trail that the legendary Sir Edmund Hillary took when he and Tenzing Norgay completed the first successful Summit of Everest. Therefore, I was also fearless. I hoped.

When we arrived at the Dolphin Guesthouse, the same lovely staff and owners greeted us. We slept in the same bed and probably heard the same pigeons cooing on the windowsill. We knew which café we liked to eat our lunch in, and which shop sold us the best trekking poles and the corner where the albino man tried to sell you small wooden flutes every day. The jeweller was happy to see us again, and we made friends with a family who owned the pashmina shop. They gave us sweet milky tea every time we visited. And the kukri knife man laughed as we stooped our heads to enter his shop and sat on the stools to chat. But it was the carpet shop man who literally chased us down the street in his eagerness to see us again. I imagine it was because we had been such good customers the year before. Or perhaps it was just Danny's fun nature that was so appreciated everywhere we went.

The bus ride to Jiri and then beyond to the next village, Shivalaya, was right at the start of festival time. If you think of Christmas shopping and public transport in Australia, then times it by 100; you have festival time in Nepal. We boarded the bus and found that the seat we had been allocated was broken. Our trekking company offered some money so that the driver would reseat us. Danny and I squirmed when this happened. My Nepali language had not progressed since our last lesson with Saimon, and the *'tapaailaai kasto chha?'* had even slipped our minds. We tried to hide behind our backpacks when the owner of our new seats arrived with his ticket, and the bus driver demanded that he take another one. When you read this, you may think this reeks of privilege. And it is true. It remains one of those times that when I remember it, I am not proud. Then the bus departed reasonably on time to the scheduled departure, and we set off for the 11 hour drive towards Jiri.

At first, I thought the bus was full. All the seats were occupied. Not long into the drive, the bus pulled over, and a young man who had been hanging out the open door called out, 'Jiri, Shivalaya!' several times. A couple more passengers boarded and found space near the back. Within minutes the bus stopped again. The same thing happened.

'Jiri, Shivalaya!'

More people boarded the bus. This continued until the entire aisle was full of people. *Now the bus is full*, I thought.

But it wasn't. We stopped again and again. With each new passenger, their luggage was thrown on top of the bus. Each time we wondered if anyone had taken our luggage in the hustle of activity. We were jammed into our seats. Things got really bad when a man nearby began to fall asleep and lean on my shoulder. He leant on me so heavily that after some time, my shoulder ached. I shoved him off me, then Danny and I switched places. A new passenger arrived and somehow managed to sit himself down on the floor between Danny's legs. He also fell asleep, and as he did, his head dropped into Danny's lap. I could not stand it anymore and called to him to wake up. He groggily looked at me and shuffled into a new position without a word. We were fast learning that our western sense of personal space was uncommon in Nepal. Eventually, we arrived at our destination, and there was Saimon ready to trek again. We caught up on each other's news, then slept, eager for our second attempt at reaching Gokyo.

We walked in rain and mud, up and down for the first seven days. Then, just as Danny said it would, the skies cleared as we reached Namche Bazar. We met new trekking buddies Jeremy and Tracey from the USA, which made the mud and rain more bearable. An encounter with a leech also added value to our time with our new friends.

Earlier that day, we shared our story of the leech in our friend Kerry's eye. The leech was lodged in the corner of her eye and although small, resisted us as we prodded and pulled at it, before realising that salt was the best solution. It happened during one of our training hikes, back in Australia, and until that time was our best leech story. However, later that evening, we heard a commotion coming from our trekking buddy's room. Upon investigation, there sat Tracey with a leech far up her nostril, happily sucking away; getting fatter by the minute.

Our days of walking through mud and jungle had finally caught up with us. Leeches love wet, muddy trails, and love climbing onto unsuspecting trekkers. Attaching themselves to interesting body parts, all with one intention— to suck our blood! It's not life-threatening, but that doesn't stop a person freaking out when they discover the growing fat slug-like insect gorging themselves on our precious life source. Tracey was not impressed, but the rest of us were quite amused by the leech's choice of suction. Of all places, why the nose? But after our initial wonder, we got to work sourcing some salt to shove up Tracey's nostril, knowing that once the leech felt the salt, it would release its jaws then Tracey could blow it out. Tracey suffered a slightly swollen and irritated nose for several days after. Saimon enjoyed the entertainment, and the guest house owners found a new use for salt.

After the first week passed, we reached clear skies of Namche. The temperatures dropped, and we again noticed the effects of the altitude. By the time we were approaching Gokyo Lakes, deep snow had covered the tracks and the slopes. The snow gleamed and glistened in the sunlight. We made it to the village of Gokyo, one of the highest villages in the world. We saw the three sacred lakes and ate more fried noodles. But I felt terrible. A stabbing migraine had developed, along with all the other altitude sickness symptoms; extreme tiredness, difficulty processing information, and clumsy motor skills. Normally, there are no medical supports in Gokyo. However, on that particular day, an Australian nurse taking part in a study program on Acute Mountain Sickness (AMS), happened to have hiked from Machermo to Gokyo that same day. Danny and I went to see her. She took my oxygen levels, asked me some simple questions, and observed me trying to walk in a straight line. She concluded that I had moderate AMS and recommended that I take a Diamox dose and consider going down lower immediately before nightfall. But she also offered the idea that perhaps the medication would improve my situation, and I may be able to stay the night. That left me to decide: Do we retrace our last 3 hours of steps, returning down to Machermo? Or do we wait out the night and hope I improved? We would need to hurry, as the longer I stayed, the worse I felt, and the closer to sunset it became. My head hurt, my stomach reeled with nausea, and I was fatigued. Compelled by the knowledge that, should I worsen during the night, a walk in the cold dark was a bad option. There was only one choice for me. I led the way with Saimon carrying my bags, Danny carrying his own, and we covered the trail in less than 2.5 hours, arriving in Machermo just as the sky darkened.

After instructing Saimon not to look for the cheapest rooms, just the warmest, we dumped our walking poles, packs and gloves and found a cosy spot in the dining room. We devoured hot noodle soup and chapati, drank lemon, ginger and honey drinks, and several Mars bars. Satisfied, we set up our sleeping bags with water bottles, head torches, and medication within reach. Then drifted into the type of dream-filled sleep you have at altitude. Our photos tell the story of beauty, and my memory tells me of the struggle. I was grateful for that nurse who just happened to be at Gokyo that day. Both Danny and I felt strongly that it was a blessing and a provision for me. Not everyone has such a great outcome.

When we got back to Lukla, we visited with Saimon's sister, Didi, again. Except that this time she was quiet. The teahouse didn't shine with her smile, and as we left, I had a feeling that something was wrong. I asked Saimon about it, he told me that she had been very unwell in her stomach and that "no-one was fixing it."

When I was 13 years old, I decided to become a Christian. It was at a High School Hall on a Saturday night, the 1st of May 1982. I responded to a challenge to recognise who Christ was and what he had done for me. I had spent the last 31 years committed to that decision. And while I had known what Christ had done for me, I was still discovering what I would do in response to that.

There had always been a nagging sense that I was meant to do something significant with my life. Weren't we all? A bible verse from Luke 12 stuck with me, *"who has been given much, much will be demanded ..."* I had long since recognised that my life was rich with blessing and provision. Then surely much was required of me. But what did that really mean? How could I pay forward all the love, hope and faith that I had received throughout my life and make a positive difference to others? I knew I had been able to participate in that to some measure. But I longed for more. I longed to surrender to a purpose greater than mine. I longed for the divine plan to unfold.

As we carefully clambered down the uneven tiny wooden stairs from Didi's teahouse, a thought—no, a feeling—rose within me. *Pray for her.*

"You mean really pray for her?" I questioned the feeling. My heart began to beat quicker. My body temperature began to rise with the increased activity in my heart and mind.

Until this time, we had not prayed for anyone in Nepal. Apart from the blessing on Saimon when we finished our first trek. But here was a woman, of whom local medicine was not helping. I don't know what she had tried so far, but I didn't need to. A strong sense that this was something for me to do filled my thoughts, and I couldn't shake it.

I waited until Danny and I returned to our cold, tiny room, carpeted with bright green outdoor carpet, then I blurted out my thoughts.

"What do you think?" I grabbed my Bible and searched for the story that was running through my mind.

In Acts chapter three, there is a story of a man named Peter and another man who was begging near a temple. The beggar couldn't walk and reached out to Peter as he passed by. Peter looked at him and the beggar expected to receive something from him. Peter told him straight. "I don't have silver or gold, but what I do have, I give to you. In the name of Jesus Christ get up and walk." He then grabbed him by his right hand and pulled him to his feet. The beggar stood up and walked. In fact, it says that he leapt in excitement and thankfulness!

That is what I will do, I thought. *I will give what I have to Didi. I will share my faith for healing. I will pray for her. I may not be rich or important. But I have this to give.* We decided to ask permission from Saimon. We were uncertain how this request would be received and we were eager to show respect and honour. It was arranged that we would return at 3pm. We prayed for love and boldness.

As promised, at 3pm, we walked back up those tiny wooden steps, pushed back the curtain, and stepped into the room. Along each wall lay wooden benches with padded cloths and several tables laid out with random cups and bowls of noodles or rice. On the padded benches sat several men. Brown wrinkled faces with years of portaging up and down mountains showed in their eyes. All of those eyes were now on us.

Didi sat on the wooden bench between Danny and I, as we attempted to explain to Saimon that we believed Jesus was the healer, not us, and he translated to Didi. I put my hand on her stomach. I peeked through my eyelids and saw that the entire room was transfixed on us. At that moment, we simply loved Didi and asked Jesus to heal her. Then we went back to the room with the bright green carpet. And we wondered what would happen next.

It wasn't until 12 months later that we learnt of the outcome; that Didi no longer had her stomach problem. But by then, so many more things were in our hearts.

Nepal returned with us to Australia. We spoke of it to each other and to others. We printed off photos, and we wondered; what could this mean? I sensed there was more to my interest than mere tourism. But we went to work, watched movies at the cinema, cleaned our house, shopped, hiked our local trails, and held new grandchildren. Our lives continued rolling on.

Meanwhile, in Nepal, the albino man kept trying to sell flutes, the kukri knife man drank tea in his shop, the yaks grazed on the mountainside, and the breeze whispered through the juniper and whistled around the peaks. We made another plan. Next time we would trek *and* visit a local church. We booked more leave from work and counted down the days.

Chapter 4

You know when you go

By now, there seemed to be a rhythm to it. Go to Nepal. Come home from Nepal. Plan next trip to Nepal. But something new had emerged. While we loved the trekking, there grew a distinct awareness that not only our feet, but our hearts, had become involved. Our friendships with Nepali people refused to stay put when we got on the flight back to Australia. They leaked over into our lives here. We exchanged phone calls and emails. We wondered how they were doing when we heard news of flooding or landslides. And we began to meet other people who were connected to Nepal.

One of those people came into our church. In a casual conversation, they mentioned a group in Nepal called Iris Nepal, who worked with homeless men in Kathmandu. I listened and went home to email them and find out how we could meet up. Someone put a book in my hands, 'My Seventh Monsoon,' written by Naomi Reed, who had lived and worked in Nepal with International Nepal Fellowship (INF). Naomi and her family spent 6 years loving and serving the Nepali people; training Nepali physiotherapists to meet the needs of their people. I drunk in every word of the book.

Most people love a good story. But I have always been particularly drawn to stories by missionaries or explorers who believed that God had sent them somewhere for a specific reason. When our second daughter, Heather, was born, we lived in Brisbane. The house was a 1900s worker's cottage complete with an early cooker stove, sleep out, and windows so close to the neighbour that we could reach out and shake hands. Heather was a bit of a crier and not much of a sleeper. Therefore, I struggled as a new mum with a toddler, a shift-working husband, and a house that was basically just a megaphone for all noises. Once the neighbours let off expletives in our direction as we attempted to let Heather cry herself to sleep. I needed help.

I sought help in the form of old family friends who had been missionaries in the Philippines in the 1970s. Affectionately called Uncle David and Aunty Pam, they were the spiritual guideposts for many of our family members. For me, they were also the only people remotely resembling family within 2000 km. They came, they prayed, I cried, and then they left. But when they left, I felt different. Something had shifted.

Now, I know that not every time someone prays, there is an immediate tangibly felt difference. But do I believe that every time, God has heard. I believe He is working on it. But in this case, I went from depression and an endless cycle of stressful insomnia to elation and overwhelming joy. It was without a doubt as if someone turned on a tap. And one of the outcomes of that running tap of joy, was a hunger to read faith stories. One particular story was an autobiography, Isobel Khun's 'By Searching.' A missionary from Canada who spent 1935-1950 in China. Today the details of it are lost to the passing of time, but how her life story made me feel remains today.

Over the years, I read and met people whose lives made me feel that there was something that I wanted to do. Something that would mean leaving my known home, where things were familiar and easily accessible, to a new and challenging place and people. But I never dared think of myself as a missionary. I didn't think that I fit the profile. But I began to ask questions. I began to ask questions of God. I researched Nepal, and missionary societies and development organisations. All the time, phone calls went to and fro between Nepal and Australia.

"Tapaailaai kasto chha? How are you? When will you come again?"

We did go again and managed to complete the Annapurna trek with Saimon as our guide. But with an addition to our team this time. By now, we understood more of the day-to-day economic struggles of Nepali people. We asked Saimon if he had a friend or someone who could also trek with us as a porter. That's when we met Bhanu. Bhanu came from Saimon's village, Sotang, in the Solukhumbu and was newly married. His small shop had recently caught on fire, and the mobile phone and gadget business he had built up was gone in that instant. Bhanu was gentle and shy. He was also new to being a porter. Working as a porter during the trekking season in

Nepal, can mean making cash money that will support your family in school tuition, pay the rent or pay for medical treatment that you may not have been able to afford. Because of this opportunity, many young men work on the trails between March and April, then again between October and November. The months when hordes of foreign trekkers flood the popular trekking regions of Nepal. Bhanu was one of them.

The Annapurna Sanctuary Circuit trek was the same region that Danny and his family had trekked in 1982. We rested on the stone steps and stared at the same mountain peak, Machapuchare (The Fish Tail) as they had, and my heart soared. We stared at that same mountain from our hotel window in Pokhara, the resort town beside a lake, and the place where all trekkers stay before and after the Annapurna trails. We couldn't get enough of the beauty. It had been a very busy season on the trail, and each night we were uncertain if we would find somewhere to sleep. At one point, we had hiked uphill for 3 hours after lunch only to find that all the lodges there were full. Larger trekking companies and groups pre-booked the beds, which left no room for individual or smaller groups.

Despite having a registered guide with us, we did not have the clout that bigger groups possessed. We had to turn around and walk back 3 hours downhill, arriving just as the sun slipped behind the bamboo and rhododendrons. Fortunately, we convinced the lodge owner to give us a tiny room next to the kitchen and provide Saimon and Bhanu space to rest in the dining room. This lack of accommodation continued all the way up the trail, until we reached Annapurna Base Camp, where miraculously there were plenty of beds. Perhaps the snow and fears of avalanches kept some trekkers away. The 360-degree view of Annapurna absorbed us. We stood in a bowl of beauty with the glory of God on show in all directions. We went inside to the dining room and ate steamy bowls of curried vegetable noodles and felt proud. At 4130m in altitude, it might not have been Everest, but it satisfied us. For then.

Our trip back to Kathmandu was going to be by air and scheduled to take approximately 30 mins. Saimon and Bhanu were going by bus, and it would take them around 11 hours. They were unable to secure seats and knew that they would probably have to stand the entire journey. *Perhaps*, I thought, *some tourist may allow them to rest on their shoulder or fall asleep in their lap*. I had a new appreciation for why those things had happened to us on the bus ride one year before. Having a seat on a Nepali bus can be a real privilege that not all have access to when needed. After carrying someone's trekking gear for 10 days, then standing on the bus for 11 hours may just mean that you end up falling asleep on someone's shoulder. And really, this is not so weird after all.

In the two weeks after the trek, we met the church that worked with homeless men and participated in their outreach program and children's house for a few days. We felt challenged and were impacted by the neediness of the men, and the absolute vulnerability of their lives. But we did not feel that we should continue to stay in touch. We saw something and felt something. We believed they were doing something great, but we didn't see ourselves as a part of it. Sometimes you just have to try. Or as I have heard the saying – when you go, you will know. And we did.

The rest of the time spent in Kathmandu, after our trek, was quickly taken up with shopping and relaxing on the roof-top of the Dolphin Guest House. Trying to catch a glimpse of the mountains through ever-increasing dust pollution. Kathmandu valley was developing a reputation worldwide for poor air quality. The dry winter season only increased the problem. We learnt a new Nepali word – *dhulo*. Dust. We also learnt that taking a Nepali family out for a meal was fun.

For the past three years, Lama and his family had been hosting us in their home. We couldn't do the same in our tiny room with the toilet that sat underneath the shower and the bed within centimetres of the entrance to the same toilet. We had to come up with another idea. We invited them out for dinner. Not knowing what they would think was suitable, we asked them to choose. They chose one of the established restaurants in Kings Way, Durbar Marg, where shops selling brand name clothing and shoes shouldered ATM's. Where up-and-coming business families with college degrees from the USA window-shopped after buying ice creams.

Lama told us that he would collect us from our guest house. He arrived on time with his wife, Gita, and two sons, Prasim and Phrahnai. All of them were squeezed into the back seat along with another young woman. It seemed that when we invited the family, the *whole* family came, and this meant that Gita's younger sister was also included. Danny sat down in the front seat next to the gear stick and Lama, while the family squeezed a little more as I got into the back of the taxi. In total, seven of us travelled in the tiny Suzuki around Thamel and over to Kings Way. It was fun. Nothing like being so close to someone to let down your barriers and feel part of the family.

The meal itself was not memorable. Not that it was bad, nor great. The only thing we remember is that when the waiter came to the table to take the drinks order, the two children and Gita's sister all ordered chocolate ice-cream faster than you could say, namaste! And that was their entrée! Copious amounts of Coke and Sprite were drunk as we chatted and laughed our way through, momos (Nepali dumplings) rice, pizza, and fried sausage on toothpicks.

When we finished our meal, we took photos and piled back into the Suzuki taxi, making our way through the darkened streets where dogs lay in the shadows. Even the pigeons were quiet. Nepal has a knack for constantly evoking the senses. Or is it that we are constantly learning something new when travelling? At night the deserted streets, with darkened guest house windows, empty taxi stands, and roller doors pulled down, create a feeling. An atmosphere contrary to the 'normal' city bustle. And that night, no horns beeped, no puja bells rang, no rooster crowed. Just the random bark of a dog and the rare sound of a vehicle in the distance. I saw, heard, and felt the silence of Nepal.

By the time we left Nepal that year, in 2014, we had made firm friends with several families and had cemented our trekking experiences. We felt like we had two homes. One in the north of Australia and one hedged in between two huge powerful nations, India and China. Nepal. A small, developing, fragile nation just finding its democratic legs after years of civil war and dogged by political rumblings, corruption and challenging geographic contexts. Surely, there were brighter days to come. But their struggles were not over yet—rumblings of a different type simmered beneath the earth.

Chapter 5

Though the mountains be shaken

I t was Saturday afternoon, on the 25th of April, 2015, Danny was out on the veranda with my brother Rob and his wife, Belinda. We were visiting them on the Sunshine Coast for the Anzac Day long weekend. The day was spent swimming, catching waves, and walking through the state park that linked Noosa to Sunshine Beach. It was what you might call idyllic. Feeling content, I went inside to find something in the bedroom and looked at my phone. There were several missed calls from Saimon and one from Lama. *Why are they both calling me at the same time all the way from Nepal?* I thought. Straight away, I felt nervous. *What's happened?* I didn't have to wait long to find out.

International news travelled quickly of the huge earthquake that shook Nepal right to the core of her people. An initial 7.8 magnitude quake centred in Gorkha hit at around 11:15am, but aftershocks continued hours afterwards. The quake crumbled ancient temples and stupass, lifted highways, and cracked thousands of buildings. Shaking everyone from Kathmandu to the Indian borders. It destroyed family homes built of stone and wood, school buildings and infrastructure across the country, from high in the mountains to deep in the valleys. The figures at the time told a story of devastation: 9000 dead and around 22000 injured. Landslides in the villages and avalanches on Everest froze the Nepali people. They moved out of their homes and slept in open land areas, fearful of more shocks. Our friends made contact and assured us that they were ok, but talked with the language of fear. No-one felt safe.

I cried for Nepal.

We didn't return to Nepal that year. Instead, we sent over some financial aid to our friends and the one NGO that we knew of and trusted, International Nepal Fellowship (INF). Despite the earthquake, and sleeping outside, Nepal's people still needed to pay rent, buy gas, eat, and send children to school–if the school building was still standing. So, we gave. And I continued to cry. But I also prayed a lot. I remember standing at the end of our bed, in the apartment we were living in at the time, having a revelation. I had secretly been wanting to be a missionary in Nepal. I had never said that to anyone and had not even admitted it to myself. I went through the daily motions of my life in Cairns. But something was going on in a parallel life. Another life that my heart yearned for. As I stood in my bedroom, tucking the sheets around the mattress, I realised that my heart and soul were in Nepal. I was there even if I never returned. I was still sent to Nepal. There are three words commonly associated with a mission heart. A heart that wants to see the best for all people. A heart that is prepared to give and support work that will build others' capacity to live a full and abundant life. A heart that says it will go if and when required. A heart that can be described in these three words: pray, give, go.

I was praying. I was praying for Nepal, my friends, and the church that I was yet to meet. As I prayed, a plan began to take form in my mind. The first step was to learn the language. During the year we stayed home, I acquired a qualification to teach English as a foreign language, contacted INF headquarters in Nepal and began to teach myself basic Nepali. I had to start at the very beginning — vowels, consonants and verbs. I scribbled little palm cards for myself and downloaded pronunciation tips from YouTube. I began to practise by speaking with our baby grandson. One of my favourite new verbs was *sutnos*, meaning 'please sleep.' A truly helpful phrase for all parents and grandparents. Small children don't mind you practising new language skills with them, they just follow your expressions and forgive you if you use the incorrect tense. Throughout 2015, between the swims at the beach, the picnics, working at my church, and hiking the local trails, I planned another trip to Nepal. *Maybe now*, I thought, *I will find out what all this means.*

New Year's Day, 2016, we flew into Kathmandu. This time with our son Daniel and his girlfriend Breanna. We stayed at the Dolphin Guesthouse again. When we went on the rooftop to enjoy Nepali tea and some snacks, we couldn't quite see the mountains. In the space behind the guesthouse, a new taller building had risen in our absence and blocked the view. We looked at the other things that surrounded us: geraniums in pots; children cleaning their teeth out the window; and women in red saris squatting next to hot oil as they fried lentils and samosas. We watched the crows circling at sunset and heard the motorcycles edging their way through the tight corners carrying two, three and four family members. Everything was new and exciting to share with someone visiting Nepal for the first time. On our fourth visit, we felt like professionals.

Daniel and Breanna enjoyed Kathmandu. Seeing monkeys, eating yummy pizzas at The Road House restaurant, and bargaining for colourful woollen beanies. One morning, we walked from Thamel towards Swayambu, The Monkey Temple. As we crossed the Bagmati River, a Didi was walking alongside us. She came up to my shoulder in height, and gold jewellery jangled from her ears and nose. I braved it and began to address her in Nepali. She responded unperturbed, and we walked side-by-side covering the common courtesies.

"Tapaailaai kasto chha?"

"How many children do you have?"

"Are they sons or daughters?"

"How long have you been in Nepal?"

Sometimes crossing that bridge can be a smelly experience as rubbish clogs the river below. But on that morning, the connection and interaction made the walk very sweet. I felt incredibly proud and happy that I had connected with a complete stranger using some newly found common language. Who was she, this elderly woman on the bridge? I will never know. But she was warm and open, and I loved her. We shared a moment, a walk, and we shared as mothers and grandmothers. I won't forget her. I wonder if she will remember me?

After a week in the city, Daniel was ready to venture outside the city. Kathmandu sits in a valley. And when the winter weather dries out the mud in the drains, on the streets, and between houses, it turns to dust. The taxis fling it in the air, and the buses puff through it as though it were clouds. The dust lifts in the breeze and resettles again, unable to rise out of the valley. This had been a problem for years, but had increased with the excess rubble and fallen buildings caused by the earthquake. Dust and dirt are not Daniel's favourite things, and the noisy city bustle can be quite stressful at times. It was the trek that he and Breanna were really looking forward to.

As soon as we landed in Lukla, the sky was blue, the forest green, the air fresh, and the pathway quiet. January is not a very busy time in the trekking season, so you don't have the same number of trekkers trying to pass you. Or the competition to get in first to order their dal bhat or fried potato and egg at the lunch stops. It really was a very leisurely time together. Although we didn't attempt to go any further than Namche Bazar, at 3440m, we could still see the big-name mountains—Everest, Ama Dablam, Nuptse, Lhotse and more. In the afternoons, we ate chicken sizzler and drank hot lemon and honey in the Tibet Guesthouse. We searched for yaks above Namche in the area surrounding Khumjung, where the dry brown plants with tiny leaves cover the slopes, and the yaks graze and roam freely. Their large bells making a deep, slow ring as they try to keep out of sight. We followed the bells, catching glimpses of their long furry tails poking out of the juniper bushes. Sometimes it felt like they were playing a game of hide-and-seek in our attempts to get close to the animals.

Returning from the trek, Kathmandu was dark. The challenges caused by the earthquake obvious; the city lay exposed in the aftermath. Not only in the building ruins and the rubble, but also in the hotels and tourist restaurants. Gas was in short supply and the load shedding program, which Nepal had been suffering under for years, was at an unbearable level. Load shedding was how Nepal managed what they called a lack of energy to supply the whole country with electricity around the clock. A schedule ensured every street and village took turns to have power for certain hours a day. For years this had been in place, and we noticed it regularly when we had first started visiting, 4 years earlier. It now seemed to be around 20 hours a day without power. Because of the inconsistent supply of electricity, people had been cooking with gas for years. And now, since the earthquake, this had become an even bigger problem. India had reacted over certain political and power issues and set border blockades into Nepal. That meant that much of Nepal's supplies of gas, rice, petrol, etc, were not being delivered. You could almost hear the Nepali people's groan as they pushed through to sleep, eat, and love at that time.

Winter dragged on. Dark, cold and expensive. Our friends told us of paying up to 4 times the usual price for a bottle of gas, only to find that their money had disappeared and no gas ever arrived. Our room in the Dolphin sat in darkness; winter clouds obscured the sun and warmth. Our favourite restaurants didn't serve the same meals, and even Lama's taxi struggled to get fuel. Across the country, Nepal struggled. Despite loving them, we had no way of affecting the situation for the better. We decided to cut our visit a week short and head home.

Cairns, warm, green, and familiar, awaited us. We made our way up the street, passing the ordered electrical wires on poles. Inside our house, we switched on the light, popped bread in the toaster, and turned on the air conditioner.

How easy it all was.

Chapter 6

Why Nepal?

Because of our fast exit from Nepal, during the cold January of 2016, many of our plans were left undone. One of those plans was to meet Ashok and his church family. This had been organised through emails over a few months. Ashok's name had been given to me through an Australian mission organisation called Australian Christian Churches International (ACCI). While I had been busily enquiring about possible connections that our church had in Nepal, Ashok's name had come up. So, I emailed him. His responses were warm and friendly. Later, Ashok greeted me over the phone with laughter and a sense of humour. I immediately sensed that I would like him, and I knew that there would be another visit, with time to meet up. So, I waited.

Since my first visit to Nepal in 2012, my initial quiet sense of purpose that I felt had become a constant loud voice in my heart and mind. I thought about Nepal daily. I probably thought about it hourly. Why? Why Nepal? What was it that made me think I had to do something? And what really was the thing? That was it. I thought I had to do something in Nepal. Sure, I wanted to share the epic mountains and colourful streets with friends and family. But there was something more. I had a strong feeling that I could initiate something, a project that would positively affect Nepali people. But I had no idea what. What I did know was that the years of making friends, learning the language, and returning each year meant something. It meant something to Nepal, and it meant something to me. My faith told me that prayer changes things. It changes me, and it changes opportunities. That year, I had been praying about what and how this 'something' could become a 'real thing.'

Four things happened next. Somewhere around March, I was driving to church one morning, talking to God about my future, about how to make the 'something' happen. I guess I was trying to put some pressure on God to do something. As if God would respond to pressure! But I was having a respectfully candid chat with Him about these things. I was about to head into the roundabout on the Trinity Beach exit. I know exactly the place when those words came to mind. The grass beside the road was overgrown from the wet season, the Sunday morning traffic easy, as I slowed to take the corners.

Then it happened. A clear phrase came into my mind. A phrase that had the accuracy of an arrow hitting a target. I knew it was smarter, wiser, and more intuitive than I could be.

"My doors are automatic doors; they open as you approach them."

Ever since I was young, I was aware of the tremendous power that the gift of choice contained. Every choice we make holds a consequence. The consequences can be simple or profound. When God told me that His doors open automatically as we approach them, He talked to me in a way that I understood. He wanted me to know that I had to move, and then He would open doors. Without stepping forward, no door would open.

Even though Danny had been the one to initiate the first visit to Nepal, I was now the one with the intense passion for returning. When I told Danny that I wanted to go back twice in the same year, this time it was he who wasn't interested.

And fair call.

I worked a couple of days a week for our church on Pastoral staff, and Danny had a fulltime job as an Aircraft Engineer.

His time off was limited.

Mine was flexible.

When considering to take action in a particular direction, it is incredible how many things begin to confirm the path ahead.

The second thing that happened was a conversation in a friend's café. Richard owned a great café called Sing Sing. It was located at the end of a laneway in Cairns, and you would often find people you kind-of-knew sitting there sipping and chatting at the kitsch tables and stools. This one morning, I wandered in and became part of the scene. I and Martina, an experienced traveller and someone who you feel you can share your thoughts freely with, got talking. For some reason,

I blurted out what I had been secretly considering for a few weeks.

"I want to go to Nepal for three months later this year – alone." I held my breath. There I had said it. Now was I going to do what I said or just take back the words and return to my wonderings?

"Sure, you can do that. Three months isn't long," Martina said.

She will probably never know how profound that brief conversation turned out to be. She could have put out the fire. But she didn't. Those words gave the idea oxygen, and from there, I made concrete plans. My next step was to have a chat with the most significant person in my life—Danny. Three months away was going to be a new experience for me. I needed wholehearted support. Anything worth doing in my married life has been done with the agreement of Danny. And for that, I am incredibly blessed. We make a great team. Of course, Danny agreed.

So, now I knew that I was going. And once I blocked out that time in my calendar and told everyone, I suddenly began to get clarification about some other things. For some time, I had been considering the concept of a group or network of women who assisted other women. Particularly, women in Nepal. One of my friends, Susan, who was more like a big sister, died the year before. She was wise in so many ways. I had this sense that she was an inspiration for this cause. I even had a name for it—Wise Woman Project (WWP). The name came to me while descending my local walking trail, Lumley

Hill. I held that name in my heart and meditated on it for months. What would it look like? What would it do? I needed to get some more clarity surrounding the details before it could happen.

Now, it does seem that all my big ideas happen while I am walking up and down hills alone. And I would say that about 80% of the time, that is true. But I do spend a considerable amount of time hiking. So, it makes sense that if God wants to speak to me or get my attention, then when I am hiking alone is a good time to do it.

The third thing that happened occurred while walking with Danny. We were rounding a corner an hour into the walk, about halfway down the Green Arrow track, when I began to tell him my idea. My idea to create an initiative that would assist Nepali women to live fuller lives, through the support of women here in Australia. I somewhat nervously asked Danny what he thought. I asked him if he thought I was crazy for thinking that I could do something like this. His response was, and is, the confirmation that I needed.

"Why not? Why couldn't you do it?"

And, so I did.

I planned an event.

I created a logo.

I asked a local artist, Celina, to compose a live painting portrait from a photo that we had taken in Nepal years before. This photo had always stuck in my mind as the face of our project. The image portrayed an elderly woman dressed in red, wearing turquoise jewellery, sitting outside a temple in Durbar

Square, Kathmandu. She sipped tea from a cup as the people wandered in and out of the temple. We snapped her photo from across the square. Sadly, we never got to ask her permission, years have passed since then, and she has become the face of our charity. Back then, I was unaware of how important that photo would become.

As the date for the launch event drew closer, so did the date of my departure. The day that I was going to launch the event on social media, I was so nervous. I called a friend and told her about the plan. Until then, I hadn't told many people. When I am attempting new things, I take my time to share the news with others. It is a measure of self-protection. But it is also a measure to protect the vision. The more important I believe it is, the closer I will keep it to my heart. I see that it is a principle in the Bible also. Mary, the mother of Jesus, "treasured up all these things and pondered them in her heart (Luke 2:19)" as she grappled with the growing understanding that her son was Christ, the Messiah. From that verse, I learned that it is ok to hold things close to your chest. I think that protecting the vision or the dream is wise until the right time to reveal it.

I had two dreams over the two nights before I launched WWP. This was the fourth sign. In the first dream, I was having a baby. This was definitely not my subconscious desire for another child. But, in the dream, the baby was a girl. Everything was fine, and I delivered with ease. The next night I dreamt again of having a baby. This time the baby was a boy, and while everything was fine, he began to grow right before our eyes. He grew so much without us even having to do anything. The hospital staff wanted me to leave the baby there for a night so I could go out for a date with Danny. But I didn't want to go and leave the baby with other people. I had a strong sense that this was my responsibility and that I was not at peace for someone else to take over. I believe those dreams were God speaking to me and letting me know that there were multiple parts to the call to Nepal. I understood that WWP was like a baby of mine. One whom I was required to watch over and nurture. And it would grow.

I now knew for sure that WWP would birth from idea to reality. I knew this was my course to take. I sensed this was my calling. I did not know what would exactly happen in Nepal. I had a few plans. One was to teach Drama to school students with a local project called School of Performing Arts Kathmandu (SPAK). This work took place in public schools where the arts were not accessible for many children. Because I had a background in theatre and education, it was a great fit and provided me with some structure and certainty for my three months. But certainty was probably not the right word when it came to working in Nepal.

Our event launched with 60 women in a groovy café in Cairns, Flying Monkey. We ate yummy dahl, met new friends and watched as Celina worked on the painting that I dubbed 'Aamaa' —Mother. When we secretly auctioned the painting, both Danny and I had submitted the same amount on our offer – $600. Neither of us had discussed this, but we were excited to be the owners of the painting. It makes sense now that we should be the ones to have it hanging in our living area. Aamaa is beautiful, gracious, wise, and resourceful. I see her every day, a constant reminder of the people that God called us to love and serve.

There were so many really cool things about that event. The best thing was seeing that others would join you if given the opportunity to support something lifechanging. They will rejoice, and some will even commit to sacrificing or investing in it. Those women who did just that have continued to be the same people who have made WWP the financial blessing that it has been over the years.

A few weeks later, I flew out of Brisbane, kissing Danny goodbye, a large suitcase full of expectation and a heart alive with the imagination of what could be.

Kathmandu lay waiting.

Chapter 7

The Open Door

T he same sounds that I had heard over the past 4 years, from the third floor of the Dolphin Guesthouse, woke me.

Cooing pigeons.

The gentle tinkling of puja bells (worship bells).

The fruit seller calling out, "*Syaau, keraa, syaau, keraa!*" (apple, banana, apple).

Indistinguishable conversations in the courtyard below.

"Aah, I am here," I smiled to myself. Rolling over, I grabbed my usual things needed to begin the day. Sitting up in my firm bed, I wrote in my journal and gazed out the window. Here I was, on my own in Nepal, with ten weeks ahead and no set itinerary. This was probably one of the most exciting things I had ever done in my life! I was thrilled to be here. I was thankful and full of hope for the potential opportunities that could arise. But my first step was to eat breakfast, then make arrangements for where I would live for the next three months.

Breakfast didn't start until 8am at the Dolphin, and I simply could not wait that long for a coffee every day!

After one week of living in the Dolphin Guesthouse, I realised that getting coffee early in the morning wasn't the only issue. I needed more room and something a little further away from the bustle of the busy tourist area of Thamel. After checking online, I found a one-bedroom rooftop apartment with a full kitchen and private bathroom in an unfamiliar area of Kathmandu. On the day I went to inspect the apartment, I walked through an alleyway lane adjacent to the building and saw a European woman with two small boys. It was intriguing to me that she should be there in a non-tourist area with her two children. We smiled at each other and began to chat. She informed me that she was, in fact, living in the ground floor apartment of the same building that I was interested in. Her name was Christine. She warmly welcomed me to see her apartment and filled me in on what it was like to live in Kathmandu solo parenting. Christine was German and had been in Nepal for around 3 months when I met her. She fast became one of my closest friends there and remained that way over the years.

I looked at the rooftop apartment and quickly decided that it was exactly what I needed. I walked back into Thamel as the sun was setting; the dust swirled around in the traffic, horns tooted, and thousands of Nepali feet hurried home to cook more dahl and rice. I almost skipped with joy at my new adventure—the anticipation of the unknown unfolding with each step along the broken footpath. I felt a great sense of being alive and was filled with such thankfulness and amazement that

I could have such an opportunity to do what I was doing. I was passionately, actively responding to what I had been called to do, living with purpose. The next day I moved out of The Dolphin and into room No. 5 of Four Red Doors Apartments.

On the afternoon that I moved in, I climbed the four sets of stairs to room No. 5, and met a very large monkey at the top step, sitting in the doorway. The monkey's arm was elbow-deep inside a massive jar of noodles, attempting to eat a snack. I think I must have screamed because the housekeeper appeared, yelling at the animal to move. The monkey was as startled as I was and promptly escaped through the open window above the couch. I was then given strict instructions to always close the window when I left the apartment. This was exactly what I intended to do. 'Welcome to Four Red Doors,' the little sign with the internet password said. I already felt like it was going to be interesting.

Over the next few weeks, a routine fell into place. I rose at sunrise and went onto the roof with a coffee, watching as Kathmandu awoke. Enjoying the activity on other rooftops— children playing with a puppy; women hanging out freshly washed saris; older men trimming their moustache, and Didi's (housekeepers) sweeping the stairs from top to bottom. I never needed an alarm while staying at the apartment. The hand water pump in the neighbours' garden creaked so loudly, it ensured that I never slept past their first face wash of the day. As the weeks passed, it got colder (winter approached). I stayed inside on my couch, wrapped in a yak blanket as I listened to music and journaled, coffee in hand. After dressing, and eating some banana or egg, I walked the 6 blocks along Lazimpat Road, and turned left, dodging a taxi, scooter, motorcycle, and a dog at the corner. I headed towards Nisha's house, for my Nepali lesson.

Nisha spent three hours, five days a week, teaching me the basics of Nepali. I devoured the lessons and was diligent in completing the homework. However, many times, I grew frustrated with myself. Some days I cried, disappointed in my progress. Nisha always challenged my learning but was warm and kind in encouraging me to succeed. Over the weeks spent together, we learnt more than language. We shared our lives. We talked about our children and our struggles. We talked about our religion, family expectations, and gender roles in our cultures.

"Did you have an arranged or love marriage?"

"Why do you ring bells in the morning?"

"If I touch your plate after I have eaten, why is it considered unclean?"

"What is Christmas?

"Do you have to live with your husband's family?"

It was really challenging sometimes explaining why we do what we do. At one stage, I was able to use the whiteboard to explain what Christmas was all about. But it was mostly me doing the learning and the receiving. Nisha cooked me delicious Nepali snacks, and we zoomed around on her scooter in and out of tiny potholed side streets, through shopping markets and *jams*. She persisted in teaching me even when I wanted to give up. We developed something more than a business arrangement—we became friends. I met her family and ate in her kitchen. Both gave me such a sense of love and joy.

I completed the teaching project with SPAK. A young man, Gopi, and I teamed up to teach the classes twice a week. Gopi was a great musician and also a very kind guy. There were times that I would have been totally lost without his help. Both in and out of the class. Our classes were fast and full-on. Each class consisted of around 50 students, all crammed into a tiny room to perform drama exercises. There was little room for movement, and even less, for performance. Sometimes we moved out into the parade ground, trying not to disturb other classes. Most of the time, we failed to not become a distraction, as students from other classes hung out their doors and windows trying to catch a glimpse of what we were doing. I had imagined completing so much more with the students. But my plans were often thwarted by circumstances outside of my control. It was my first experience working in Nepal, and I had a lot to learn.

I had planned around five weeks of lessons that would finish with a performance. The overall rationale was to provide a creative expression for students who may have experienced trauma through the 2015 earthquake. The project hoped to use theatre as a means for students to tell their stories through theatrical play. To reclaim joy, fun, and expression after such a time of fear and trauma. It was a great idea, with so much potential. But we only managed to get through about a third of what I had planned. Celebrating with simple group performances that focussed on stage presence, confidence and movement. Our classes had commenced just before the most prominent festival season of the year; Dashain. Schools are closed, on and off throughout the year, for religious days. There are limited opportunities for extra classes, such as ours. But that wasn't the only thing to disrupt school, or routine, at that time in Nepal.

On one of the days planned for our classes, I got ready and walked down Lazimpat Road to hail a taxi and head to the school. I noticed that the road was unusually quiet, void of the usual chaotic traffic. There weren't even many other pedestrians walking the streets. But didn't think twice about it as a taxi pulled over. I got in and negotiated the destination and fare. Even though there are metres in all the taxis, I have rarely found a driver who uses them. Some form of discussion usually takes place about the rupee value of the ride. I was aware that my tourist price was probably a bit higher than the local price. But I always tried my best with the little Nepali language I knew. We agreed on the price and set off; arriving at the school quicker than usual. I jumped out and walked through the alleyway to the school gates.

The gates were locked.

Inside, the school appeared still; not a blue uniform was in sight. I phoned Gopi. But he didn't answer. Next, I called the organiser of SPAK. I explained that I was at the school ready for class, but it was closed.

"Oh, yes, that is because there is a banda. A stop, curfew," the organiser replied.

I had heard of such things from books I had read, but I was unaware that it was happening now. "So, how am I to know this?" I asked, rather irritated.

"Oh, you didn't know? Yes, school is closed. All Government office closed also."

I got even more irritated. "So, if you knew this, then why didn't you tell me? You know I can't read Nepali or understand much. I just paid for a taxi here for no reason…" I wasn't being very nice now.

The organiser remained silent.

"Next time, can you just check if I know, please. Thank you." After that, I was silent too.

Not only had I missed the message about the strike, but I had also missed other messages. Messages that were less obvious but important nonetheless. The inconvenience for me was not something to get angry about. Plans that changed were not something to feel offended about nor raise your voice over. I learnt something that day, riding back in another taxi. I looked out the window into the quiet streets. I thought about how my culture and lifestyle was so intolerant of inconvenience. It is generally thought acceptable, even expected, that someone would get cross or complain if plans were inconveniently changed. If bus schedules ran late, shops closed unexpectedly, the electricity went out, or the internet dropped out. These were all viewed as very inconvenient in Australia. In Nepal, these were every day occurrences and were the least of the problems for many millions of people. Lack of clean running water, gas to cook with, accessible healthcare, and food security were everyday concerns. My little inconvenience that day was not so bad. I decided to see it that way. Not only then but every day. Later that evening, I felt very grateful as I sat on my couch, wrapping the yak blanket around me tighter, and practised my vocab for the next day's class. How blessed I was. And I hoped to remember it more often.

Along with Nepali classes, practising speaking the language I had learned so far with Nepali shopkeepers, and teaching theatre, I also had a very active social life. One of my friends from Cairns, Tim, had arrived in Kathmandu three months earlier and was working as a project manager for a hydropower start-up company. Tim and I caught up regularly for coffee, dinner, and enjoyed a glass of wine in a new café right in the centre of Thamel. We would message each other sometime in the afternoon, walk from our respective homes, or wherever we were, and meet at the 'Café with No Name.' Here a European couple had set up a groovy little wine and snack bar. All the profits went toward supporting a children's home, that was established after the earthquake. It was a quiet and friendly spot to start off the night, and the added bonus was that it supported a great enterprise. It was also nice to find good wine in Nepal.

There were several churches that we visited in those months. Some of them were English speaking, others were multilingual. I met several pastors who were keen to partner with me to do ministry and development work. After years of wondering what I was called to do in Nepal, there was suddenly no shortage of opportunities. But it wasn't that easy.

With whom do you partner? What is the best thing to do? How will I know if it is right? But most of all – who do I trust?

The reality was this: I was an Australian woman, on my own, in a country with only basic language skills and no real knowledge of cultural or societal differences. I didn't even know what I didn't know. What I did know was that I expected the right doors to open as I approached them. So, I stepped forward. Carefully, prayerfully, and expectantly.

And the doors opened.

Chapter 8

You do it for me

I stood out everywhere I went. I tried to dress in Nepali fashion. Still, I was taller than most people and whiter. In a country crowded with millions of brown eyes, my green eyes bore a beacon of difference. Outside of the tourist area, I was the source of curiosity in most settings. How did it feel to be different? Sometimes it was a nice feeling—a feeling of being special. Most of us like that. But if being different gives some kind of privilege, then in some ways, that felt wrong. Being different may mean that I receive attentiveness or service faster or better than most people in the same context. It also may mean that I am offered assistance when others are not. This could be kindness and understanding of my vulnerability or ignorance at its best. But at its worst, it could be out of preference because I hold some image of power, wealth and status. It can be difficult to differentiate. There really is no way to fully know. I just had to try to remain humble and resist all sense of entitlement.

Regardless of the reasons, it seemed that everyone was eager to partner with me in various projects. WWP was in its infancy and had no set projects to begin working on. The aim of spending ten weeks of networking, and exploring potential opportunities, was to go back to Australia with a plan for the work that would be done. As the weeks rolled on, I was beginning to wonder if that would happen.

Around week 6, I was invited to join a family to visit some of the smaller villages in the Terai. These villages are the plains of Nepal, about a day drive from Kathmandu. Here we conducted women's church gatherings and met with the pastors and leaders. I had gathered some funds from our church in Australia; Danny and I also contributed to the costs of 5 days spent on the road and assisting local pastors. Even though it was women that we went to meet, there were always men in the meetings as well. In all three of the communities, I was told that I was the first foreign woman speak there. The hearts were open, warm and expressive. I heard many heartfelt stories of how their lives had changed for the better since finding faith in Christ.

I met a special, elderly man who had been crippled, but after believing in Christ, regained the use of his legs. He looked at me with watery eyes, standing shoulder height to me, and told me how his whole village came to Christ. Since then, he visited neighbouring villages daily to share his faith and testimony. Without payment, he gives all of his time. Venturing up and down the hills, encouraging and praying for the new believers. I looked at his simple clothes, his dusty feet and his treasured Bible. Many of the inhabitants in that area never had the chance to attend much formal schooling. But new Christians will persist in reading the Bible until it makes sense to them. Such dedication to something that I have often taken for granted.

Before I left Australia, I dreamt of something that could have been taken as a warning. In the dream, I was in a foreign country. As I went into a public toilet, alone, I was assaulted by an unknown person. The dream threw me, and at the time, I didn't know it's relevance for me. But I prayed that I would be wise in my travels. I don't think that all dreams have to, nor should be, applied to reality. But if that one did, I can think of one meaning.

By the time I finished those 5 days on that particular road trip, I knew that I did not want to work with that ministry again. The details don't need to be retold, but I had felt vulnerable and alone in the situation. I learnt from the experience to be wise about who I conducted projects or ministry work with. I decided that from then on, I would not work with anyone I did not know unless there was additional support from a trusted third party. I had always been so accustomed to having Danny alongside me that it was a big learning experience to become wise enough to handle things alone. I didn't always do what wisdom offered. Because of this, others and I suffered at times.

Those few months alone in Nepal challenged and changed me. In my life, there were times when I have been too trusting. Times when I didn't look ahead to see where things might lead.

I have always been great at jumping at opportunities. I just needed to learn to listen and see what God had to say about them.

Then, finally, I met Ashok, the person I had been planning to meet for 12 months. Tim and I met up for our Saturday morning program of church and then lunch. Church in Nepal is on a Saturday. I used to think that was because all Nepali Christians were Seventh Day Adventists, but since learnt that is not the case. The true reason is that Saturday is the only day considered a 'day off.' Schools and offices open every other day of the week. Surprisingly to me, Ashok invited me to preach for his congregation that week without even meeting me. Tim and I managed to find our way to the *chowk* (intersection) near the zoo. We waited on the side of the road at 9am looking for someone to collect us. As the dust from the tires of motorcycles and jeeps clouded over us, I covered my hair and face with a scarf, hoping that the morning would go well. I had decided to tell the story of my faith journey and use it to encourage all listening. The message was that belonging to a church doesn't save you; only Jesus can. I hoped that the meaning of this basic, yet personal, message would easily translate into Nepali.

Soon, Ashok met us, and we were taken to the church where we joined the prayer meeting and experienced the warm love of Bethsaida Church. When it was time for me to speak, I rose from the plastic seats against the back wall, then walked down the aisle. Women sat to my right, men on the left, all cross-legged on a maroon carpet. My bare feet were freezing, and I became very aware of my legs. Even though I wore a skirt that ended at my calves and a long-sleeved polo neck top, I felt like my legs were exposed. And they were. Every other pair of adult legs I passed were fully covered all the way to their feet. *Note to self: when preaching in Nepal, always choose to dress in the Nepali style*, I thought.

But whatever I was wearing wasn't a problem as I began to share, with tears, the story of my own salvation through Christ. After the service, I prayed with many women worried about the same things that I was worried about; their children, husbands, and health. Some of them just wanted to grow in their faith or to be encouraged by me. It was new but familiar at the same time, and I felt the glow of being where I was meant to be.

I gladly popped my shoes back on when we stepped outside into the sunshine. Tim and I both agreed that the church felt genuine and open. I had arranged with Ashok to visit one of the partner ministries later in the week—Vision Rehabilitation Centre (VRC). A residential facility for recovery from drug and alcohol. I was invited to take part in their weekly fellowship that Thursday night. Without any particular idea on what it would be like, I agreed and prepared a short message to encourage those in the program. A long drive from the other side of Ring Road to Satdobato in Lalitpur took me near VRC. I waited for someone to meet me and ferry me on a motorbike, down the winding streets across semi-rural paddocks and finally stop outside a set of solid metal gates. Three knocks and the gates opened to reveal the round smiling face of Parasu, the director of the program.

Once inside, a neat courtyard surrounded by bright blue simple buildings greeted me. Shon, the other director, introduced himself. We sat down together in the office to drink black coffee and get to know each other. Parasu and Shon had started the rehab in a single small room 8 years earlier, having come from a lifestyle of addiction themselves. Their story impacted me as I saw before me the dramatic change and transformation that had taken place. Their gratitude to Christ, who they credited as delivering them from the chains of addiction and darkness, was obvious. I loved spending time with them and wanted to know more. But it was time for the fellowship to begin.

We joined the men in a larger room, found a spot in the circle and sat down on the thin carpet. Someone was playing the guitar; someone else sat on a box using it as a drum. The men sang with all the volume of opera singers. Some of the songs were sung to melodies I knew, and I joined in the joyful choruses. At some point, they sang a version of the Lord's prayer. Their voices rose even louder, their faces pressed toward heaven; it crushed what remaining composure I had. I cried in wonder and a fresh sense of humility. *We are the same*, I silently cried out. *There is no difference between us. We are all brothers and sisters, because Christ died for you and me alike.* I was now kneeling with them as we worshipped in unison. What if this was why I had come? What if this was it? I could be satisfied with that.

After the meeting finished, I talked with Parasu some more. During the conversation, I asked where the women's rehab was.

There wasn't one.

"But what happens to them?" I asked.

"They sometimes come to the big metal gates and bang on the door and beg us to let them in and help them. But we can't."

Driving home in the now dark Kathmandu, I thought about those women who begged to receive help. Back in Australia, help was accessible through government or church funded programs. There would be medical and social security when things got really tough. There would be hope. Here in Nepal, I couldn't see any, nor did I know if there even was any.

It was nearly time for me to return home. I was walking down Lazimpat Road, after my Nepali class and talking to God. I was thinking about the rehab centre and the women not receiving the help they needed. Apparently, there was land for lease adjacent to the men's centre. Parasu had told me about their vision to develop it for a women's rehab. The lease would need around $5000 to get started on this vision. Could it happen? Could we do that? I became aware of my steps. I remembered the automatic doors that open as we approach them. I took a leap of faith, and with the very next step, I said:

"God, I can do $5000. We can raise that. We can believe and begin."

I called Danny, and his response was clear. "We have always wanted to do something that is the first one – or something that no-one else is doing. The first Christian drug and alcohol rehabilitation residential program for women to be established in Kathmandu! Yes, we can do it."

Monkeys were eyeing off my kitchen window when I got back to No. 5 Four Red Doors, and I messaged Ashok.

"What do you think about Wise Woman Project supporting the development of a girl's rehab?" I asked.

"Yes, that is a very fine idea, Sarah Didi," he replied.

And so, we committed to that 'very fine idea,' and our partnership with Nepal was established that very day!

Did I ever think it would begin with a drug and alcohol centre? Honestly–no. But we had a close family member who had been healed of long-term drug addiction through the love and support of a Christian rehab program in Australia. Our gratitude for that inspired us to do something and help others in the same way. With the words of Jesus running through my mind:

> *"The King will reply, 'Truly I tell you, whatever*
> *you did for one of the least of these brothers*
> *and sisters of mine, you did for me."*

(Matthew 25:40).

We stepped forward, and the doors swung wide open.

Chapter 9

What did you do in Zanzibar?

Back home in Cairns, it was raining. It had been raining for most of the ten weeks that I had been enjoying an adventure in Nepali sunshine and walking through new doorways. Meanwhile, Danny had been going to work, mowing lawns, cooking and going to work again. He had done all this on his own. While he never begrudged my happiness or opportunities, he still sometimes struggled with the routine of being employed for 28 years at the same job in the same town. Our time apart had been difficult for him, and my return did nothing to ease it. The freedoms I had experienced had not been his to share and enjoy. It was a testing time for him for many reasons. I quickly decided that a break from his norm and responsibilities was required. So, we made plans to use his long service leave to give us a chance to spend time together and alleviate what had become mundane with something fresh.

Danny is one of the best advertisers for trekking in Nepal. While I am happy to talk about it, Danny's passion truly shines as he tells everyone, "You could trek in Nepal, anyone can do it!"

While I had been teaching drama, visiting Lama, and learning Nepali; Danny had organised a group of 8 people to trek in Nepal at the end of that year, including our grandson. And I was going to be the trekking group leader! I was excited about the prospect, and had all the right contacts to make it happen, but was slightly awed with the responsibility. Probably uppermost in other people's thoughts was the question, "Why are you taking your 7-year-old grandson into the Himalayas?"

Here is why.

The year before, I had been driving Jacob (our eldest grandson) home from prep. At the time he was 6-years-old. I think I had recently returned from a trip to Nepal and he was asking all about it. Suddenly, he boldly asked me to take him with me when he is 7. I briefly turned around (I know that you shouldn't do that when you are driving) and promised him that I would. I knew then that I had to make it happen. I would take him to Nepal—the land of mountains and yaks. And in 2017, that time had come.

"So, will I go to school on my birthday, or will we go on the plane to Nepal in the morning?" Jacob asked confidently as his 7ᵗʰ birthday approached.

"Mmmm, you will have to wait a few months longer, until it finishes raining in the Himalayas and until Nanni and Grandad fly there. We will be waiting there at the airport for you." I explained.

Cathy, one of our closest friends who loves a good adventure, offered to fly with Jacob to and from Nepal and meet up with us for the group trek. What a fabulous friend she is! This meant that we had to be in Nepal on November 27th to meet everyone else in the trekking group.

For 'normal' people, that would be easy. Book a flight for a certain date and get on the plane. However, because Danny works for an airline, we have access to cheap standby tickets. This is the reason we can comfortably afford to fly regularly, but it has a downside: sometimes there are no last-minute seats, and you have to wait until some become available. In most cases, that simply means waiting for the next flight. But every so often, it means waiting for days. Days, waiting in a place you would prefer to leave; you may be ill; be out of money; feel unsafe; have to return home by a certain date; or have accommodation bookings that you will need to pay for even if you don't get there.

We have experienced all of the above.

Part of our journey that year passed through airports where security was intense, and our standby tickets didn't make sense to the border and immigration staff. It was particularly challenging in Egypt. As we attempted to depart the country, we caused a scene by trying to go out of the terminal and back into the city to find a hotel. We had not been able to secure a seat on a flight to Lebanon, and had been stuck in the terminal all day without access to money, food, water, or toilet paper! We had resorted to waiting for the cleaner to leave her trolley briefly, so we could quickly stroll passed, and grab a handful of the precious supply. Thankfully, theft wasn't added to our transgressions that day.

Apparently, no-one can leave the international airport out the same doors they entered. The only way to exit is by aircraft after being processed through immigration. It is a one-way journey. No doubling back! Police yelled at us, and men in suits arrived. Security and armed officers crowded around the growing group, all focussed on us. It took several hours of multiple conversations and, finally, a guided walk through the back of the airport. Behind immigration and border control offices and desks, through corridors that we shouldn't be in, eventually, we ended up coming through the Arrivals hall of Cairo airport. Considering that we had never actually left, and our passports would show that, we were grateful for the security guard who escorted us through that tricky situation. We knew we could not risk that happening again the next day. We quickly purchased full-fare seats and departed without any drama the following day. So much more relaxing, but probably not as noteworthy.

However, something very noteworthy happened in Zanzibar.

It was at the start of our four-month itinerary. A very loose itinerary, due to our standby tickets, and our desire to follow spontaneity rather than a schedule. Bearing in mind the one thing we had to commit to—arrive in Nepal by November 27th. The plan was to spend one month in South Africa. But first, we had 7 days to fill. I had always thought the sound of Zanzibar was intriguing. It turned out that we could fly from

Johannesburg, through Nairobi, and onto Stone Town, the capital city on the island of Zanzibar. Amazingly, we managed to do all that on standby tickets.

Zanzibar is surrounded by sapphire blue waters, and the constant threat of pirates marauding the shipping lanes from Somalia. Actually, that part is more to do with my imagination than reality. Having recently watched the film *Captain Phillips*, I was acutely conscious of that risk. However, in reality, that was not a problem I needed to worry about as I was not on a ship. I was staying on land in a 4-star resort. Nevertheless, Zanzibar has a dark, ugly history.

Until 1873, Stone Town was the centre of the East African slave trade. Being a British colony at the time, it was an act of parliament that forced the abolition of slavery in 1834. The parliamentary campaign was actioned by an evangelical Christian, William Wilberforce, and one of his associates, David Livingston, a missionary. However, it wasn't until 43 years later that the British government convinced the Sultan of Zanzibar to cease the slave trade. On our first day, we walked on the same soil that had soaked up the blood of the slaves. Knelt on the altar of the Christ Church, where the whipping post had stood all those years before. There stood the Cross of Christ, a reminder of his sacrifice—whipped, crucified, and treated as a criminal, an outcast. He was rejected by mankind. As I stood there, I thought about those things. What it meant for those who had suffered so much on that island. Those whom mankind has closed their eyes to. And I thought about what it meant for me now.

In what way do I stand by and let forms of slavery still take place around me?

In what way do I contribute to the ongoing buying and selling of vulnerable people?

But even more importantly, how can I be a part of someone's freedom?

I was inspired by the story of William Wilberforce. But wondered about the 43 years that followed, as people were still trafficked across the continents. How many more suffered because leaders delayed in doing good? There is a proverb that addresses this:

> *"Do not withhold good from the deserving when it is within your power to act. Do not tell your neighbour, 'Come back tomorrow, and I will provide'— when you already have the means."*

(Proverbs 3:27,28)

I silently prayed, *God, please help me act on behalf of others when I can, and not hold back, waiting till a more convenient or easier time. Help me to keep stepping forward and see those doors opening. Not for me but for those who need it.*

Now it was time for some real relaxation. We left the west coast and crossed over to the other side of the sandy island, about 3 hours away. After spending 6 days in Pongwe Resort, a small relaxing, slow-paced beachside oasis, our driver and local guide met us, and we began the drive back to Stone Town. We had been driving for about an hour. Danny and I in the back, the two local men in the front. Many people walked alongside the narrow road, carrying their shopping or goods to sell, much like we were used to seeing in Nepal. We were travelling at around 60km per hour when I noticed a man carrying a large firewood bundle on his shoulder. He was walking on the right side of the road then abruptly turned to cross in front of our vehicle. Our driver pressed the horn, but the man only ran faster across the road, almost overbalancing with his load as he hurried on. The driver braked sharply. But we still hit the man square in the middle of the road. Firewood flew through the windscreen. The sound of a body thudding up and over the back of the car was sickening.

"Jesus!" I screamed, ducking behind the front seat. Somehow thinking that the broken bits of firewood were body parts of the man, broken on impact.

The car came to a stop. We all sat frozen. I continued to speak the name of Jesus. The driver and the guide said nothing for what seemed like ages. Then one of them finally spoke, "Stay here, do not get out of the car."

They left us there. Quickly we prayed, "God, just be here, just be here."

Our thoughts then turned to the situation that was escalating outside. Groups of people were filling up the side of the road surrounding the car. The windscreen was smashed, bits and pieces of wood strewn over the dash and seats. We spoke to each other calmly but decisively. "Don't do anything. Just stay here and wait." We both knew that this could go bad very quickly.

Zanzibar is a predominantly Islamic society. Even though Stone Town and the resorts are very welcoming of tourists, we were definitely a minority. Our white, English speaking, Christian demographic had never made us feel more vulnerable. Had we been in Nepal in the same situation, we would know what to do. We would know what to expect and who to call. We even had some language on our side. But, in Zanzibar, we felt very alone. We had only been there for a few days and knew nothing of their legal or justice system. What if there had been an existing feeling of anger toward tourists, or foreigners in general, among the villages? What if the man is dead and they want revenge or some sense of justice? We stayed quiet and still.

Waiting.

Someone put their face up against the window of the car and looked through the dark tint. Until that moment, no-one knew that we were in there as the tinted windows had kept us hidden. Shouting and more people gathering around followed. We rechecked that the doors were locked and resisted making eye contact with the curious faces pressed against the windows. Twenty minutes passed, and the guide returned with another man. They told us to get out, gather our bags, go with the new man–an off-duty police officer, and get in another car a bit further up the road. Not knowing what else to do, we followed. As we walked along the road, we passed the man's body. He lay twisted on the side of the road, surrounded by weeping women. Danny tried to explain to the guide that someone needed to turn the man on his side in case he was having trouble breathing. No-one listened. We were hurried to the waiting car, keeping our eyes down and avoiding the bystanders' stares.

We were taken to a spice farm, which had been our original plan, en route to Stone Town. During the spice tour, and still feeling shocked and numb, two police officers approached us with our guide. They asked us if we wanted to help the man. We had already decided that we would be cautious. We were well aware of the strong possibility that a bribe would be expected if we showed any signs of uncertainty.

"You help the man?" They continued asking in a few different ways.

We maintained that we did not know which man, or what they meant. After some time, they gave up and left us.

"I gave them some money so that they don't make a charge," our guide then quickly told us. "Don't tell anyone about today, don't tell the hotel, please." That was precisely what we had planned to do.

Once back in our hotel, I picked up my phone. Intending to make contact with our family just in case something further should happen. But, unusually, there was a new text message on my phone. Until that time, I had not received any messages on my Australian SIM card. We always used the internet to communicate when travelling internationally. Yet, somehow this message was receivable. The message was from a new acquaintance in our home church and read:

> *This morning as I was praying, your face came to mind, and I prayed to God for your safety and for His blessing, love…*

The message was sent at the very moment that we were travelling in the car, about to hit that poor man, and be alone in that potentially dangerous situation. God had prompted someone back in Australia to pray for us. I was overwhelmed with that knowledge. Also, with the knowledge that the woman, who was a fairly new believer and a new friend, was so in tune with God's plan that she responded, prayed and sent me a message. And that single message came through when no other messages ever had; it had to be God.

We called our son and explained the situation, then we got the first seats available out of there on a flight back to South Africa. As I stood at the immigration desk on exit, the officer fired questions at me. I immediately felt nervous.

"What did you do in Zanzibar? How long were you here? Where did you stay?"

But I needn't have worried, he was just being friendly and taking the opportunity to practice his English.

As the plane took off and turned towards the mainland of Tanzania, we gave thanks for our safety and prayed for that man, whose life was now quite different. We prayed that he would be healed, that there would be provision for his family, and that the driver would not be punished. Most of all, we prayed the people of Zanzibar would know the true freedom that William Wilberforce knew. Freedom through Christ, a freedom more precious than any other.

Chapter 10

Horns and Travel Hacks

During 2017, WWP continued raising funds through selling Nepali made products and receiving donations at local events. The money raised went toward two projects. Firstly, to Girls Rehab Centre, which by that time, had purchased land and progressed to the building phase. WWP, after checking plans and having discussions with people like Tim, Ashok, and our engineer son-in-law Josh, decided to go ahead with supporting the building of the residential rehab centre. This meant that I was often busy overseeing fundraising activities and ensuring that the money kept funding that vision. While it felt very money focussed, I was confident that the act of our generosity spoke more than we could ever know.

The second project that WWP sponsored that year was a two-day health and hygiene seminar for women in the rural area of the Terai. Around 100 women attended and received basic health information that they and their families could implement immediately. The information provided began with lessons on cleaning, rubbish removal, safe food preparation and storage, safe toileting practices, and progressed to sexual and reproductive health. This opportunity for the women to attend such an important seminar, prepared especially for them, made a huge impression. For many of the participants, this was the first time they had attended something organised exclusively for women. Here they were able to ask questions and discuss personal subject matters without the usual attendance of men.

In April, I squeezed in a quick visit to Nepal. During this visit, I spent a week with a large Christian community in Nawalparasi. This church was founded around 50 years earlier by one of the first generations of Christians in Nepal. I had the honour of spending time with the gentle and humble pastor while he recovered from surgery. When he asked me to pray, share some scripture and encouragement with him, I felt quite shy and humbled. Here I was, coming from a relatively free and easy life, where my faith was practised without obvious challenges or persecution. There he was, in the Terai of Nepal, after years of persecution and struggle in building one of the oldest, and biggest, churches in the country. I prayed with tears in my eyes. During that week, I was given many opportunities to speak in churches, youth meetings, home meetings, development projects, pray for the sick, and teach new believers. My Nepali language skills grew, and I experienced life in my first Christian Nepali home. Once again, I was the first foreign woman to speak in their churches. I have to say that honour never gets old.

But in September and October, while we were spotting rhinos in Africa, visiting friends in Germany, and riding camels in Egypt; the girls' rehab building was nearing completion. We arrived in Kathmandu with one week to spare before our grandson was due to fly in. Because we had a few free days, we decided to take the opportunity to do some trekking training and visit Saimon and his family in the Solukhumbu village of Sotang. I had spent 3 days there the year before. I was eager for Danny to also experience the lifestyle of a Himalayan village, away from the tourist areas.

We took a 10-hour jeep ride from Kathmandu to Nele; stayed overnight, then continued in the same jeep for another 3 hours the following morning. Before we got in the jeep that morning, I taught two English classes in the local school. It was fast and fun. I taught them how to greet friends in the Australian way, and the difference between formal and informal English. Around 60 children in Nele now know how to say 'G'day' like a true Aussie, thanks to a very brief and crazy English lesson.

I was still explaining what a 'mate' was when our jeep driver sent word that they were ready to start driving again. So, I ran down the hill, through the village, jumped over the running drain, and carefully balanced along a wooden plank to meet the jeep. The engine already whirring. Squeezing into the back seat with 2 other people, and 6 other passengers spread across the front and luggage area, we bumped across the roughest roads I had seen in a while. Our packs, pressure cookers, potatoes and peanuts jostling atop of the jeep. Inside, we swayed around corners, leaning into the bends as the deep ruts of dried out mud sucked the tires downward. The jeep rocked and lurched from side to side, ready to tip over at any moment. I held my breath as my head bumped against the window with each rock of the jeep.

After hours of the 'extreme driving' experience, we stopped at a tiny rough-looking tin shelter sitting precariously on a cliff ledge. It seemed there was nothing to prevent the shelter from disappearing over the sheer drop to the valley and river below. The road ended. From there, we had to continue on foot. We gathered our packs and picked our way step by step, down the rough track toward the suspension bridge high above the Dudh Kosi River. Suspension bridges are common in Nepal. Whether you are on a popular trekking route or going from one village to another on the other side of the valley – you often need to cross those bouncing, jiggling bridges. The bridges are usually towards the bottom of the valley, lower to the river. This means that when you go down to the bridge on one side, you will have to go up the other side of the valley after you cross. Somewhat breathless, and unaccustomed to carrying my own pack, I was relieved to see Saimon waiting for us halfway across the rocking suspension bridge. He quickly insisted that he carry my pack. We crossed the river and began the uphill climb to Sotang. Welcome back to trekking legs!

We enjoyed the fresh air, the views of the Himalayas, and the unique lifestyle of a Solukhumbu village. Sotang is a bit of a central village for the district. They have two schools, a weekly market, several shops, two small restaurants/tea shop, and a fairly young church. For 4 days, we ate freshly killed and cooked chicken curry, buff curry and momos, and pancakes. We practised Nepali with the children, and I taught English in both the public and private schools in the district. Danny also managed to get us invited to the church, where we shared our testimonies and prayed for the sick and elderly. At one point, Danny was praying for a sore shoulder when the man responded, "Oh, it is getting hot, and it feels like a fire in my body now!" We can only attribute that to the effect of the believer's prayer in response to the promise in scripture:

> "...they will place their hands on sick
> people, and they will get well."

(Mark 16:18)

Our time there was invigorating. The school and church asked us to stay for three months. We refused apologetically, explaining that our grandson would arrive in a few days and we had to meet him in Kathmandu. We walked back to the river, crossed the bridge, and deciding not to repeat the drive across the dreadful road, we walked through pretty hills, flowers and farms instead. Then the 10 hours jeep ride to Kathmandu. Feeling worse than jet-lagged, we arrived in Kathmandu at 7:30pm, to a busy jeep hub on Ring Road. Hailing a taxi, we tumbled into the vehicle.

"*Lazimpat Road, kati parchha* (how much)?" We tiredly mumbled, then I think I dozed off.

It is always exciting to arrive back in Kathmandu, no matter how long I have been gone from the city. Our first job was to settle into apartment No. 3 at The Four Red Doors: check that no monkeys were in our kitchen, and that the hot water was switched on. The hot water was certainly more of an issue than the monkeys were. Hot showers are still a fairly new luxury in Nepal. Not that they don't exist, but it can be a bit hit or miss whether you get one or not. Solar is popular, but not always efficient. Gas hot water systems are usually the best and safest method, but even those can be temperamental. Probably issues to do with the installation rather than the actual hardware. The idea of a running showerhead streaming with hot water is still unusual to many Nepali and very uncommon in rural homes. As foreigners, we often expect the same level of priority given to hot water as we have back home. In reality, if I wanted the same as at home, why not just stay there? Therefore, when I am in Nepal, I have to appreciate and celebrate the differences. We tried to shower, but it wasn't hot. We did our best and went to bed, wanting to be ready for our trekking group to begin arriving the next day.

Darren and Liz were the first to arrive. They also travelled on standby airline tickets but gladly arrived on schedule, excited to explore the bustle of Kathmandu. We sent them off with Lama and his taxi on their first day, which may or may not have been a good idea. It was great in the sense that they got to immediately immerse themselves in all the heritage and cultural sites around the valley, accompanied by the smiling face of Lama.

Lama welcomed them, putting Darren in the front seat next to the gear stick and close to the horn. The horn plays an important part in driving in Nepal. We had become accustomed to the incessant beeping of horns from daybreak until nightfall. Lama was particularly good at using the horn. Often giving Danny the job of 'Hornblower' as a joke. Lama was probably anticipating that Darren would also enjoy that role. With Lama, they joked and laughed their way around Patan, Durbar square, Bhaktapur, and back to Thamel. The downside to that was the traffic. I distinctly remember waving goodbye to Liz and Darren in the morning; everyone was relaxed and happy. But the returning faces were a little tauter. The disordered and hectic traffic was a bit stressful; to top it off, the view of someone doing their toilet business by the roadside did nothing to help. Fortunately for us all, we were able to debrief about it and alleviate any concerns. Our new visitors had quickly learnt that Kathmandu was a diverse and struggling city, both rich and poor, all making their best attempts to get by. We looked forward to getting out of the city and into the mountains.

Within a few days, the whole group had settled into Kathmandu. Jacob had made his way from Cairns to Kathmandu via Singapore under Cathy's fun and safe guardianship. Saimon arrived from his village, and we had a group meeting in the lounge area of our apartment. I did the introductions then sorted out accounts and tickets to Lukla. The trekking permits had been arranged earlier. All we had left to do was the last-minute purchasing of water bottles, poles, and snacks. It wasn't long before we set our alarms for the early morning taxi ride to the domestic terminal. There is always the routine of preparing on the night before; emptying my whole pack and rechecking all the gear. Then I carefully put lip balm, tissues, a small plastic Ziplock bag, and around 5000 rupees in my small pouch that sits across my body. The pouch is within reach at all times. The head torch and ibuprofen sit at the top of my day pack, for easy access no matter the situation.

There are several trekking hacks that I have developed over the years. My top tip for women is this: carry a small plastic sealable bag in your pocket, or pouch, where you can place used tissues, toilet paper or sanitary items in the event that you don't toilet near a rubbish bin. There is nothing unsightlier and disgusting than toilet paper or tissues scattering the trail, or worse, in piles left near uncovered faeces. There is always a way to cover your 'business,' and disposing of material waste. Carrying your paper trash with you to a more suitable place of disposal is simple respect for the environment, fellow trekkers, and the people who live and work in the area.

The second hack is about your head torch. Always carry it at the top of your pack. Always check that you have pushed the lock button on the switch, to avoid it being bumped in transit, and have back-up batteries on hand. We also carry a steriPEN for water sterilisation, a pen-sized UV light that destroys 99% of the nasties found in untreated water. We have spare batteries for them also. It may sound like overkill, but it is best to carry a canteen that can be filled and sterilised throughout a trek. Buying water in plastic bottles creates extra weight, then the need to find a means to dispose of them somewhere on the trail. Rubbish is a mounting problem in the Himalayas, which both tourists and locals have contributed to. Choosing to carry reusable items over disposables, where possible, is advisable. Pack checked, and all items accounted for; we were ready to go.

The next morning, as is often the case, the Kathmandu runway was closed due to fog and cloud. No flights were taking off. We were delayed for hours, waiting along with hundreds of other trekkers and guides in the departure area, drinking expensive but not-so-good coffee, and trying not to get anxious. Although Danny and I did not have a strict timeframe for our trek, everyone else did. They had return flights booked and only a certain number of days to complete the trek. Time is an important element in acclimatising, so it isn't wise to rush or cut out days, especially on the way up a mountain.

Jacob sat on the floor of the departure terminal, colouring, while I talked among our group and reassuring them. A family of four had joined us from our hometown, Cairns. We had known them since our teenage years. It was exciting for them to join the group, and make this epic journey with us. Their plan was to head to Everest Base Camp. Cathy, Darren, and I would attempt to reach Gokyo. Danny, Jacob and Liz were going to be our base team and stay in Namche for the week, keeping at a lower altitude. To manage a safe separation of teams, Saimon had brought along his brother, Bikkas, as an assistant guide to accompany my group. Bikkas had trekked with us the year before. We felt comfortable knowing that

Saimon was just a phone call away for most of the trek and that I had hiked the trail twice before.

At around 11am Saimon rushed over and explained that no flights would take off for Lukla that day. To reduce the delay further, he suggested that we depart by helicopter instead. Although it would cost around $USD 50 per person extra, we were all glad to be on our way. Half of us climbed into the first helicopter, and we took off over Kathmandu. As the helicopter gracefully turned, I looked down through the glass panel beside my feet. Thousands of colourful buildings dotted the green valley below as we soared upward, over the lower peaks toward the Everest region. Jacob squirmed next to me, excited and already a little tired. He snoozed until we landed, and stepped out onto the familiar tarmac, halfway up the valleys, already deep inside the Everest Region.

Chapter 11

One Foot in Each

B y the time both helicopters arrived in Lukla, our group had drunk several pots of hot tea, and eaten plenty of fried eggs with potato. It was around 3:30pm when we all finally set off toward our first destination. We had all been awake since 4:30am that morning, and had a stressful few hours awaiting a cancelled flight. We were now dealing with a level of cold that all of us were unaccustomed to. Each of us was already out of our comfort zone. But the main pressing point, from my perspective, was the fading daylight. There was only an hour and a half until nightfall, so I knew that we couldn't relax yet.

Jacob especially felt tired. He soldiered on with the excitement of a 7-year-old, but it was a challenge as the minutes ticked on. The walk toward Phak Ding should take around 3 to 3.5 hours to cover the 8.2 km trail length. It was the first Himalayan trek that our group had experienced, so we tried to take it easy. However, the ever-present thought about walking in the dark with a group of new trekkers, which included a child, pushed us to keep a steady pace.

Although I don't remember feeling overly stressed, I must have been. After around 30 minutes of walking, I needed to find a place to toilet. My stomach must have been storing anxious tension in preparing the group and getting us onto the mountain. Now that we were finally there, my body started to relax. Saimon managed to find someone willing to let me climb down their rough staircase and enter a dark, wooden room, perched off the side of a steep slope. I found relief. You never know how exciting toilet adventures can be until you travel through rural Nepal. I remember that several years previously, I had needed to use that same toilet. While relaxing in the dark, my eyes became accustomed, and I saw strips of drying meat hanging next to my head. Food for the next few weeks, no doubt!

Continuing our journey, we settled into our walking order. The two younger girls, 15- and 17-year-olds, were in front alongside the porters. Their parents were behind them, then Cathy, followed by Darren and Liz. Lastly, myself and Danny with Jacob, with Saimon in the rear, always ensuring that no-one was left behind.

As the sun began to disappear behind the mountains, it got significantly colder. One by one, we all stopped to put on jackets and gloves. For some, this was easy. Just unclip your day pack and pull out your down jacket. For others, it meant digging around for some time, taking gloves off and putting them on again. All the while, sensing that we shouldn't be standing still for long. Firstly it was freezing; secondly, it was getting late. After we were all adequately clothed, we pressed on. But it wasn't long before we needed to stop again. This time we needed to retrieve our head torches. Danny and I quickly found ours and Jacob's, positioning them in place. Saimon, and a few others, easily got their torches ready too. Unfortunately, some of the group either could not find their torch or discovered that the batteries were already flat and had no spare batteries available. We shared what working torches we had; Saimon offered his to someone else and used his phone for light instead. We then managed to pick our way onward to Phak Ding. Trekking hack no. 1 confirmed. Be prepared. We arrived in good time despite the dark, cold, and tiredness.

After settling into our cold rooms in Phak Ding, we all headed into the dining room ready for hot drinks, food and an early night—ready for the next bright, beautiful and somewhat challenging day, uphill to Namche.

Our trek that year taught us all a lot. It didn't matter how many times a guide may explain that the plan may not end up being the reality; it will always be a big deal when the idealised version doesn't pan out. Sickness, weather, or any other thing out of your control may mean that you cannot make it to the destination that you want to reach. This is something that you should be prepared for. But it doesn't mean that it makes it any easier. Trekking at altitude in cold conditions with new food, and environments, creates unpredictable responses in people. Sometimes, fear is the problem. Sometimes illness. Sometimes it is simply that you have had enough and want to return to the comfort and warmth of your hotel in Kathmandu. Sometimes there isn't an answer or reason; it just didn't work out. You have to hold onto the idea of a plan loosely, considering that the plan is just that—an idea.

The way the Sherpa culture perceives the mountains is different from my western culture. We see the mountain as a thing to be conquered. Sherpa believe that the mountains have to give you permission to climb or to summit. My western mind perceives a mountain to be something separate from myself. It is a physical object. However, other cultures hold a different worldview, seeing all of nature as holding spiritual identity and relevance. After years of watching and learning with my Nepali friends, I have slowly begun to see this difference not as wrong, but as something different to respect and try to understand. I do not hold the belief that a mountain has a spirit or a power. But I do recognise that others think so. I believe that the mountain, trees, birds, and sky are connected by the fact that they all display the beauty and love of a creative God. It is God who is powerful. When things on the trek, or in life, don't work out as I had thought, I find consolation and understanding in that, and it makes me think of this verse in the book of wisdom, Proverbs:

> *Many are the plans in a person's heart, but*
> *it is the LORD's purpose that prevails.*

(Proverbs 19:21)

We completed two weeks in the mountains. We all saw Everest, multiple other peaks, yaks, mountain pigeon, alpine forest and sparse dry, dusty trails lined with juniper. Some of us made it to our destinations, others stayed put in Namche, knowing that it was enough. Others attempted their very best, but had to return back to lower ground. Some of us saw monasteries and sacred lakes. We all learnt new card games, and whether we really did like to eat dal bhat every day, or not. It was harder for some than others. Some of us got colds, others got more seriously ill, requiring medication and assistance. But we all grew in some way. Our lives mingled with Nepali porters for two weeks. We took photos together and shared jokes about each other. Then we flew back to Kathmandu. After a few days in the city, we would be separated by different flights back to Australia. We said goodbye.

I learnt so many things during that trek. One thing, in particular, was about myself. As we departed from Namche, in an attempt to make it to Gokyo for my third time, I was scared. I would be leaving Danny in Namche. My usual guide, Saimon, would be working with the other group heading to Everest Base Camp. I remember crying as I walked through the winding lanes in Namche Bazar. *God help me to lead our small group even though I don't feel brave at all*, I prayed. I knew what was coming. I knew the cold, the altitude, the tiny uninsulated rooms, the repetitive menu and the long nights, struggling to relax and breathe. And the distance that it all was from home. Suddenly, I had a thought: *buy yourself some new warm gloves and a beanie from the trekking shop. You will be ok.*

I did. I felt bolder.

It was the first time I had trekked without Danny. I found that I had a strength and courage that I had never harnessed before. I prayed a lot. I sang a lot, and I walked very slowly. I recited Psalm 121 to myself repeatedly. It became a song in my heart. It seemed to me that the psalm was written for those in the Himalayas. Have you ever noticed how many references there are to mountains in the Bible? Perhaps it is just me.

> *I lift up my eyes to the mountain—where*
> *does my help come from? My help comes*
> *from the Lord, the Maker of heaven and*
> *earth. He will not let your foot slip—he*
> *who watches over you will not slumber.*

(Psalm 121:1-3)

I enjoyed the company. Cathy and Darren were fun, but also knew the power of silence. There were many times when all three of us just walked on, saying nothing. Just breathing and allowing each other to be in the moment, admiring the immense majesty of the mountains.

There are two moments in particular that I have to mention. One occurred in the morning in Machermo. Cathy and I shared a room, and we had both developed very unpleasant chest congestions. When you spend prolonged amounts of time with someone in a small space, you become aware of each other's unbecoming behavioural habits. The morning routine consisted of many of those behaviours. The least charming was the coughing up of green chunky mucous from our chests every morning. As we struggled to get a good breath between laughing and coughing, we knew that we were bonding on another level. Often, we were right next door to Darren, so I'm sure he heard everything. At night, as we wriggled into position under sleeping bags and extra blankets, we would tap on his wall to check if he was ok. At times, we all felt a little off, so it paid to check in on each other. Altitude sickness can come on rapidly.

Then there was the dancing. I think it happened at Dole, near a quiet guesthouse in the valley. I remember the woman in the kitchen, admiring my UGG boots (Australian lamb wool boots): my secret weapon against cold feet in the guesthouses. That night, after our dinner, the three of us left the warmth of the dining room and crossed the grassed courtyard to our rooms. It was a clear, full moon night. The mountains were silvery white against the deep dark sky. Thousands of stars twinkled overhead. It was freezing as we clapped our hands to keep them warm. I don't remember who started it, it may have been me, but we began to sing, 'Dancing in the Moonlight,' the 2009 version by Top Loader. We sang and danced; it was so freeing even as we puffed with the high altitude. I'm a great believer in creating memorable moments with others. We said goodnight, and as quick as we could, we escaped the minus Celsius temperatures, sliding into our thick down sleeping bags. High in the Himalayas, we slept soundly under the blanket of stars.

Once back in Kathmandu, everyone needed to find somewhere to do laundry. A little way down Lazimpat Road, just past the corner where you can catch a taxi, there is a tiny little laundromat where you can leave your laundry and return for it the next day. It is perfectly washed, dried and folded in neat piles for you. Darren soon headed off with two bags of smelly trekking clothes. After some time, as the rest of the group were meeting up for our last group dinner, Liz mentioned that Darren had not returned from the laundromat.

"Oh," I checked my watch, "that's been over an hour and a half."

We all attempted to reassure Liz, but it did begin to feel a little concerning. Darren didn't have a phone, and did not really know his way around the area. It would be quite easy to walk past our alleyway and not find the apartment block at all. We gathered near the corner of Lazimpat Road, waiting. Several taxis pulled over, hoping for a fare, but we were not ready yet. Someone was still missing! It was getting late, and we needed to head into Thamel for dinner. Suddenly someone noticed a white head in the adjacent barber. There sat Darren, almost fixed to the barber chair, receiving a vigorous head and shoulder massage. His face, beard and head freshly clipped, trimmed and coifed to perfection. After all, he had been there for almost 2 hours! Liz was livid. A few unprintable expressions escaped her lips as she rushed in to hurry Darren up. In his defence, he had been innocently getting a haircut, not realising that, as a foreigner, he would be given the luxury gold star treatment that would take hours. And of course, once you are in the barber seat, it is hard to leave. He did look rather fine. I can still remember his fair head bobbing up and down as the barber leaned into Darren's back with his elbow in an excruciating manipulation.

Our trekking group returned to Australia; Danny and I still had time in Kathmandu. We had the usual farewell dinner with Lama's family; tea with Pramisa and Keshav in the Pashmina shop; and a final visit to the girls' rehab centre. Earlier that month, we were given the honour to officially open the building. We looked forward to seeing young women begin their journeys of recovery and transformation through the work of Vision Rehabilitation Centre (VRC).

Arriving home to the heat and humidity of a Cairns summer is always difficult. While Nepal was freezing, Cairns was sweltering. But it isn't only returning to the heat that is hard to manage. With each period of time, spent in Nepal, I find it a little harder to flow back into life in Australia. It's not that I don't know how to do life in Australia. I was born there. I have my whole family there. I own a house, a car, and have a job there. I belong to a church and have plenty of friends. So, what was this? This feeling of being temporary. With each trip to Nepal, people would welcome me back.

"How long are you home for?" They eventually started asking.

I began to think that maybe it wasn't just me feeling like being in Australia was temporary. Other people were feeling it too.

I wasn't quite brave enough to ask my family what they thought or saw. I guess I didn't want them to explore how they felt. Knowing that their mother or daughter or wife might want to be somewhere else. Somewhere where the colours are so vibrant, they nearly hurt your eyes. Where the fruit seller cycles under your window and shrieks out, *'keraa, syaau.'* Somewhere where the hissing and snorting of rice cooking under pressure and spices searing in hot oil, coating the air with aromas and stirs the appetite of 26 million people at 10:30am every day. Where the water isn't safe to drink, but the friends you make are like family. Where the dust of Kathmandu clings to your hair, but the ancient bazaar intrigues you, and you can't keep away. Where the thrill of learning the language surpasses the challenges of bargaining in Nepali.

I don't know if I really want my loved ones to know that I love Nepal that much. That I miss it immensely when I am not there. That I think about it multiple times a day. That every plan I consider for the future is always laid alongside my love for Nepal. But despite me not asking them about it, I think they already know. They know why I prefer curry restaurants over French ones now. They know why I sometimes wear colourful and interesting clothing. Why I pierced my nose and why I stay up at night practising vocabulary and sentence structure from a little book called, "Basic Nepali for Beginners."

But I have come to this conclusion, the difficulty lies in two areas. The first is the area of geography and culture. I love the contrast between Nepal and Australia. Both culturally and geographically. After you spend considerable time in a new place, it is amazing how quickly we can adjust—our behaviour and thinking changes. One particular example that I can think of is the first time I really noticed how few people talk with you in Australia. In Nepal, strangers talk to strangers all the time. If you stand waiting for a bus, in the bank, in the tea shop, sit next to them in a jeep, or are purchasing fabric for the tailor to sew you a *kurtha suruwal* (women's pant and top set) or a shawl. Chatting with strangers happens all the time. It happens as soon as you walk out the door. People are everywhere, sitting on the steps, in the doorways, at the teashop, and watching small children play.

Danny and I have always been quite chatty with strangers. It possibly comes from being forced to make new friends in new countries as children. Danny moved to Rabaul in Papua New Guinea with his parents when he was 11. I moved to Pittsburgh, USA when I was 17. I think we both developed interpersonal skills that have proven to help us in our adult life enormously. We deliberately seek out local people to talk to when we travel, and find that this is one of the greatest joys of travelling. It is the thing that we notice doesn't happen so much in Australia. People drive their own cars into their carports, roll down the door and shut the gate. The gardens are fenced, and no-one is seen until the next morning when the roller door comes up, the car reverses out and heads off down the street. The streets and homes lie empty all day.

I have a friend who moved to Australia with his friend. Both men were from India. In their first job, they worked hard in farming and fruit picking for several weeks. They immediately felt lonely because no-one spoke to them. They gave up fruit picking after some time, totally exhausted. They then stayed home all day, watching tv and wondering where all the people were and how they would make any other friends. One of them decided he could not take it anymore and returned to India, too lonely to bear it. The one who remained has since met a lovely girl from India, married, and has a family of his own here in Australia. But he remembers well the intense loneliness he felt in those early months of isolation in Australia.

The second area is the feeling of being happy to be in Australia, but always having a sense of longing for Nepal. Yet when I am in Nepal, I have a sense of longing for my family, my soft bed, hot water on tap, driving long distances in a short time, and understanding the news and public notices. Blending in. Funny how standing out is wonderful sometimes, but sometimes it makes you wonder. You wonder if your Nepali friends are your friends because you are Australian, and all the benefits that entails, and not just because you are you. If I had nothing more than them, no more money, education or my passport, would they be so interested in me? I really hope so. I really do. I call them my friends.

The longing for two places simultaneously is challenging. We left Kathmandu's chilly winter. Upon our return to Australia, December 2017, we settled in again for another long hot, wet summer, and focussed on our relationships in Cairns. Investing in both Nepal and Australia, straddling two countries – one foot in each.

Chapter 12

Pramisa's House

Over the next two years, Nepal became my second home. It became necessary for me to find a few affordable and comfortable places to stay while there. I had already made Four Red Doors a base for hosting trekking teams. But, I also wanted somewhere I could be with a family when I travelled alone. One of our first friends in Nepal, the Dhitals, offered me their rooftop room and bathroom in Naya Bazar (New Market). The Dhital's lived close to Thamel, the tourist district, and was walking distance to several of my friends' homes. I could enjoy sharing life with a Nepali family while still having my own space and amenities. I agreed to live with the family and settled into the room. I loved the space with a view and a private bathroom. So many things about staying there were really special for me. It must have been something to do with having the time to appreciate simple things. Time to watch the city, to hand wash my clothes and ring them out before hanging them dripping on the lines strung across the corner of the roof. Taking the time to appreciate the smell of cooking from hundreds of kitchens, to hear the children and older women talking in the doorways below. Naya Bazar was not only a shopping area, where you could buy cauliflower, chillies, rice alongside children's shoes, phone cases and fashionable denim jackets, but also a place where families lived.

Definitely, one of the other great things about living with the Dhitals was Pramisa's cooking. She creates chicken chilli and pickles exactly to my liking. In fact, everything she cooks is perfect—rice, chicken, momos, and sweet milky tea. If you were fortunate to be around for breakfast, it was always delicious and filling. Some days might be potatoes and eggs, other days doughnuts. On doughnut days, Pramisa would pass a few rupees to her son, Kritan, and he would run down the four flights of stairs, cross the road, and turn the corner to the small tea shop perched on the side of the street. Here you could find fresh doughnuts frying every morning. On Kritan's return, we would sit on the carpet around the small coffee table chatting about the day ahead, dunking the doughnuts in sweet tea. Then, suddenly, everyone would rush off to school, businesses and chores. The scooter would be dragged out of the ground floor lock-up, and off they would zip along the streets as shopkeepers rolled up their doors and the vegetable sellers arranged their goods on carts.

Right now, I am missing it immensely.

I planned two trips in 2018. The first one, in April, was to include a road trip with Pastor Ashok and Romila Adhikari to attend another of our health and hygiene seminars. These multi-day seminars were provided free of charge to women in rural communities, including both practical and spiritual teaching. It was a chance for the women to learn and be encouraged in a safe, friendly environment. All food and a place to sleep was provided for those who travelled from afar. Some women walked for hours or even days to attend these seminars. WWP had been supporting this program for some time, and I looked forward to participating in one myself.

We left Kathmandu early in the morning, driving through empty streets up and out of the valley into the warmer, greener Terai region. We stopped close to Chitwan, staying in a beautiful rustic guesthouse near a small lake. I was able to share a room with Minu. She was my buddy for the trip, and we enjoyed chatting together in both English and Nepali. I discovered that Minu was the same age as my eldest daughter, so I nicknamed her *Mero Chori* (My Daughter). It was one of the first opportunities I had to talk about life as a Nepali Christian woman. As Minu and I sat in our beds, I asked questions about her life.

How did she come to believe in Christ?

Did she go to formal schooling, and for how long?

Would she have children?

Were there particular barriers in society because she was a woman?

As I listened and she, in turn, asked me questions, I began to feel like we were equals. That we were the same. Two women, caring about the same things like family, dreams, faith and the problems of wanting something so badly but not being able to get it. Like waiting to fall pregnant or struggling with an illness. I began to believe that maybe she did love me for me. Maybe they all did love me, as I loved them—nothing more, nothing less. Just connected through love.

Around 89 women attended the seminar. This meant that all the households represented would be positively impacted by the information received. I interviewed a few women to assist me in making evaluation reports to update our supporters in Australia. I remember one particular response from a woman in her late 20s. When asked what she would change about her daily life because of the training she received, she replied, "I will wash my underwear regularly, and tell my family to do the same."

Other women spoke about a new understanding of hygiene and rubbish. Others said that they had never had the chance to learn about their reproductive system without men in the room. An elderly woman stated that she had never learnt any of the things in the seminar as she had never been to school. She expressed sincere gratitude for the opportunity.

Back in Kathmandu, I had a week free. What should I do? On the ground floor of the Dhitals' home, a rafting company stored their rafts, paddles, and camping gear. I got talking with the friendly staff one day as they loaded their trailer with gear. They convinced me that a rafting trip was what I needed. Earlier that week, I had met up with one of my son-in-law's friends, Matt, at OR2K in Thamel; a popular spot for tourists.

The menu is vegetarian, the tables low to the floor, and the vibe is funky and relaxed.

Matt had just completed a trek and was keen to catch up for a beer and chat. After being stuck in a *jam* for 30 minutes, I arrived late and sat on the cushions. I ordered a Gorka beer and hummus. A few other people from Matt's trekking group were there as well. There was plenty to talk about—trekking, Australia, the Nepali food and culture, and of course, the question always asked: 'Would you return to Nepal?' After a few more Gorka beers and laughter, we said our goodbyes. Matt was leaving the next day, but Sarah (his friend), a bubbly girl from the UK, still had a few more days. We made plans to meet again.

We ended up hanging out a few times, and I invited her to join me on an overnight rafting trip. Sarah had just completed a trek to Island Peak. A mountain peak climb that requires ropes, ladders, and crampons. I was slightly in awe of her feat, especially since she stated that she had never even trained for it. It gave me ideas for my own trekking future.

The rafting trip was fun. It was springtime, and the water although cool, was refreshing after a full day in the sun. We paddled our way downstream for a few hours, stopping for lunch and then resuming the journey along the river. It was my first experience rafting, and I loved the excitement of working together as a team to navigate the river. That evening we camped in basic accommodation just above the water level, surrounded by green grass, herbs, and far from city sounds. We were treated with all sorts of tasty food and drinks. I remember surprising the cooks with my Nepali language knowledge. But they soon recovered, and I spent an hour or so learning more vocabulary in the makeshift kitchen beside the river. At night the river gurgled past us as we bunked down under mosquito nets. I slept soundly, far away from home, away from my usual companions and in a totally new environment. I felt so alive.

In the morning, the rest of the group set off early to go canyoning. Sarah and I lazed around the campsite until it was time to cross the river and hike up to the road. We then waited for several hours under a hot tin roof at a roadside tea house. Eventually, a car picked us up and we headed back to Kathmandu, re-joining the *jams*, dust, and bustle of millions.

Every time I leave Nepal, friends ask, "When will you return?" I usually have an answer. So, as I pack, I begin to count the months until I know I will be back. To ensure that I would return, I began leaving a few bags at Pramisa's house. Storing items that I wouldn't need in Cairns – trekking poles, UGG boots, colourful kurtha suruwals and winter shawls. I had this idea that if I left things there, it would mean I would be returning again. And, so I did.

Back in my Cairns home, I began making plans with Debbie and Pierre Fourie, a couple who were keen to trek with me in October that year. I sent out an invitation to friends and contacts asking if they would be interested in joining the PEAK team for 2018. PEAK stood for People, Exploration, Activation, Kingdom. It was the trekking side of WWP. People who wished to join me in Nepal, but not interested in the ministry side of it, could participate through PEAK. It was also a way of keeping adventure finances separate from the charity finances. Only one other person signed up for the trek: Jess Earl. We decided to trek to Gokyo Lakes in the Everest Region. It would be my fourth time to hike that trail. And maybe the first time to reach the summit. The four of us made plans, booked flights, and began to train.

I had heard of something called Altitude Training in Cairns. Cairns is situated at sea level. Anywhere I usually hiked around my home would not provide me with any altitude preparation. In fact, Australia's highest peak is only 2228m, which is lower than the first day of the trek to Gokyo Lakes. Because I had already attempted to reach Gokyo Peak at 5357m three times, the idea of altitude training appealed to me. I had always struggled to acclimatize. By now, I understood that I needed to take advantage of any help I could get.

Scott, from Complete Health, was eager to assist me in my preparation. He had also trekked in Nepal and understood the challenges of altitude. The altitude training took place in a sealed room where the nitrogen and oxygen ratio level is adjusted to mimic the atmosphere of higher altitudes. It doesn't alter the pressure, as you would experience as you climb higher. But it does give you an advantage of physical fitness training. Once inside the room, you can choose to ride, do a circuit, row, or use a running machine. The first time I attempted a High Interval cycle session, I felt faint, nauseous, and couldn't wait to escape the room. After a few more sessions, I began to notice my fitness changing. Not especially while in the room, but when I was riding my mountain bike or hiking. I felt faster, and the kilometres sped by. The real test would be when I was trekking in a natural altitude above 4000m. That was where I previously began to struggle. The months ticked by. It wasn't long before it was time to set up our itinerary, finalise the mountain flights, and arrange what date to meet Saimon in Kathmandu.

Pierre, Debbie and Jess had checked off all the essential gear on the list that I provided. They had watched YouTube clips about Nepal, and we completed a few day-walks together. I was confident that we were all ready for the month in Nepal. Included in the trip would be church visits and work with the VRC. Both Debbie and Pierre were keen to spend some time with the guys in the rehab centre and share their testimony about how God had transformed their lives.

Danny had opted to stay in Australia this time, as we were already committed to visiting Nepal the following January. Only 2 months after the PEAK expedition. This time with our daughter Jessica, Adrian, and their three children. They would first spend a month in far west Nepal, Chaujahari working in a hospital with the nursing and midwifery department, through a sending agency called INA (International Needs Australia). The plan was for me to go on the PEAK trip during October/November. I would return home for around eight weeks, then fly back to Nepal with Danny to meet our family in Kathmandu for another month. It was going to be a busy but exciting time. I was excited about all the opportunities and relationships that were developing in Nepal, and how our friends and family were becoming connected with the project. The vision and calling were expanding.

But just as I was about to leave Cairns in October, our family experienced a deep, sad loss.

Should I go? God, what should I do? I prayed.

Chapter 13

Garlic Soup

We have three children. All of whom understand the importance of following a sense of purpose and passion in life. Each of them talks freely with us about what they hope for, plan for, and ultimately pray for. We are happy, with contented hearts, knowing that they include us in their lives in this way. But that closeness, at times, brings great pain as we experience their struggles and challenges alongside them. One of those painful times came upon us all during a time when we were supposed to be celebrating. Our second daughter, Heather, had informed us that she and Josh were expecting their third baby. As a family, we were happy, looking forward to another grandchild to add to our other 5. But at the 10-week scan, no heartbeat was found. It appeared that our baby had already passed into eternity.

Heather came to our home; we embraced each other, shocked and burdened with immense heartbreak. Miscarriage happens to many women every day. But that doesn't lighten the depth of grief. We prayed that perhaps the scan was wrong or that God would intervene and keep this new little life with us. That we would get to see them grow; have them hold our hand; feed the chickens, and sit at our kitchen bench. Heather and Josh waited to see what would happen. Perhaps we would be spared this loss.

After a couple of days, and more doctor appointments, my departure date approached. I was due to meet the trekking team in Kathmandu and needed to make sure that I arrived there beforehand. More scans confirmed that there was no heartbeat. We kept crying and praying; giving thanks. Thanks that we knew where our baby was. That we knew God was the God of all comfort. Heather decided that she would wait to naturally miscarry rather than have a procedure. We prayed that it would happen at the right time, and could avoid needing medical intervention. And so, Heather released me to go.

I flew out of Cairns with a heavy heart. Danny took on the role of home-based support while grieving the loss with, and for, his daughter. I arrived in Kathmandu and prayerfully got to work. There were projects to visit, friends to drink tea with, and a trek to organise. God graciously provided for us all during that season. Three days after I arrived, I was on my way to preach at Bethsaida Church for Pastor Ashok, when I received a message from Heather. She had just miscarried at home – naturally. Tearfully I read her text message. A message that I have kept with me and shared over a dozen times since:

We may not know what to think right now, we may not know what to feel. But we do know that God is always good and he is kind and he is loving.

I preached that morning with a heart of grief but a new awareness of God's loving comfort. I remember looking across the congregation. They sat cross-legged, women on one side of the aisle in colourful shawls and men on the other side following Ashok as he interpreted my story. The story of how God loves us all. The story is the same whether we are in Kathmandu or Cairns, wealthy or poor, woman or man. We all face distress and loss, and we all can access and experience the same comfort of His Spirit.

…who comforts us in all our troubles, so that we can comfort those in any trouble with the comfort that we ourselves receive from God.

(2 Corinthians 1:4)

The message was for all of us. My Nepali church family now knew me better than before through our shared distress and needs. We prayed for each other with a fresh intimacy.

The trekking team arrived, and we settled into Four Red Doors together. I introduced them to Lama, Pramisa, the kukri knife man named Sudarshan, and visited the rehab centre. There, Pierre and Debbie spoke of how Jesus had set them free from addictions and healed them. They spoke of God's love, and how he gave his son Jesus to die for us so we could lead fuller lives than any drug or other pleasure can provide. They prayed for every person in the room with tears and heartfelt words. It was a powerful evening; I felt such joy at witnessing the work of God through bringing myself, and our team, together in Nepal.

Later that week, I spoke at another church. I shared Heather's story of loss and her message of hope, explaining that God is our comforter. Pastor Prem and his wife, the founders of the church, spoke with me privately afterwards. Their daughter had just experienced a miscarriage as well, and they wished for me to pray for them all. Without hesitation, I prayed, knowing exactly what they were going through. It was a powerful reminder of how God doesn't waste anything. He promises:

> *All things work together for good to*
> *them that love God, to them who are*
> *called according to his purpose.*

(Rom 8:28 KJV)

I experienced it with my own life in a new and profound way. When we experience the comfort of God, we can then offer that same comfort to others in their time of need as we read in 2 Corinthians 1:4. I am thankful for that sad but sweet season of our lives.

Back home, Heather, Josh, and the family planted a tree on our land, overlooking the green cane fields and hills. They gave thanks and laid the little one to rest there. Danny told me about it between sobs while I sat on a couch halfway around the world, in Kathmandu.

I prayed for God to show the plans He had in store for each of us. Then I went upstairs, stood on the roof, and looked towards the Himalayas; the mountains were peacefully shrouded in dust pollution. I praised God that His presence and peace was with me there as He was with Danny back in Cairns. And He was. I felt strong enough to move forward. I left the rooftop and packed my trekking gear, determined that I would reach the summit on this trek.

It is always a thrill to fly into Lukla; the airport is considered one of the most challenging and dangerous in the world. When you land, it is normal for all the passengers to let out a cheer. Our landing was no different that day. The familiar chilly air greeted us as we stepped onto the tarmac; the enormous mountain peaks overlooked the village, the pathway leading to Phak Ding, and beyond. The porters had arrived hours earlier by foot. They had left Sotang village the day before and walked non-stop to arrive in time to meet us. After only a few hours of rest, our flight arrived; the porters were on their feet again, ready to carry our bags and accompany us on the mountain trail.

Our bags collected, and porters assigned to each of our team, we set off along the trail. Saimon was the head guide, as usual, with his brother, Bikash, assisting should any need to separate the team arise. One of the porters, Prabesh, had worked with us before, and with two new younger porters, we made up a team of 8. The trails were very busy, and the checkpoints sometimes took an hour and a half to pass through. Every trekker has to go through several checkpoints in the Everest Region, where their passports and trekking permits are sighted and recorded. This assists with statistics and ensuring that all trekkers have paid for their trekking permits. It also records every trekker that enters the region, monitoring when and where they exited, in the hope that any lost trekkers may be traced back to these checkpoints.

However, once you are two days out of Lukla, the checkpoints vanish; any record of trekkers' locations is no longer possible. That is one of our reasons to always employ a guide. At least there is someone else to assist you if you encounter any trouble. The other reason is that the employment invests in a life. This, in turn, invests in a family and a community. Each year, we check on the rates that we pay our staff and hope that it is comparable to the bigger trekking companies, or better. Sometimes, it can be difficult to tell, as talking about money can be considered rude. Over the years, we have nurtured a relationship with Saimon, and we hope that he would tell us if we are not paying enough. The fact that most of our porters and guides continue to come with us says that we must be doing something right.

We made a good team and settled into walking at our own paces. After a couple of days, somewhere between Phortse Tanga and Dole, it was obvious that Debbie was struggling. She had shown clear signs of fatigue when arriving in Namche but had picked up after 2 days of acclimatisation.

As in every other trek I had walked on that route, I found that the push just before lunchtime to reach Mong La, is quite exhausting. The altitude is just under 4000m, and while you feel hot from the effort of walking uphill to get there, you quickly chill as the wind whips around the exposed corner of the tea house. But it's a spectacular view every time and a great place to rest, eat and enjoy all the reasons why you are trekking in Nepal.

The sun was shining, warm and inviting, as Jess and I collapsed into blue plastic chairs at a table on the balcony of the Snow Lodge. I had heard my Nepali friends call the sun, 'Nepali blanket.' We allowed the blanket to cover our bodies while we ordered hot lemon drinks, garlic soup and fried potatoes. Saimon had been drilling the importance of eating garlic soup as often as possible; after years of hearing it, I was finally doing it. Even though the sun was warm, it didn't take long for the cool breeze to become a freezing chill, and we hurriedly put on jackets and beanies. It is amazing how fast the body cools down in such temperatures. Even if the sun is hot, the wind will always cause a rapid drop in your body temperature. Hypothermia was a problem to be wary of on the mountains. We devoured the hot lemon and soup while waiting for Deb and Pierre to arrive. We all took our time, hoping that the rest would improve Debbie's situation.

Refreshed, we pushed on towards Dole. Jess and I went on ahead with Saimon and our porters, leaving the rest of the group with Bikash to go at their own pace. Earlier that day, Saimon decided to continue directly from Namche to Dole, and spend an extra day there to acclimatize rather than our usual stop at Phortse Tanga. It made for a big day, and I was exhausted when we arrived in Dole. Jess and I found our rooms, then headed into the warmth of the dining room as the last of the afternoon sun rays hit the big windows. We had some snacks and warm drinks; waiting for Debbie, Pierre, and Bikash to arrive. As the sun disappeared, we became concerned. It gets a lot colder as soon as night falls, and I knew how hard it was to keep going if you were tired and cold. The altitude can really get to you then. I arranged for a porter to go back down the trail and deliver a large pot of tea and some biscuits to the rest of the team.

Finally, after an hour or so more, the rest of the team appeared. Debbie was exhausted. Bikash had actually carried her up the 'stairway of death' (the multiple steps on the trail to reach Dole) as she was unable to climb them. We all celebrated their safe arrival and made sure that everyone got warm food as soon as possible.

I recall being woken in the night by repeated knocking on our door as the bangs penetrated my earplugs. Jess and I were sharing a room across the hallway from Debbie and Pierre. I struggled out of my sleeping bag and opened the door. There was Pierre, his face tense and voice elevated. Even in my drowsy, altitude-affected state, I could tell he was concerned. Pulling on my jacket and UGG boots, I quickly went to wake Saimon. Together, Saimon and I followed Pierre into the tiny freezing room. It's difficult to imagine how cold those rooms are while I sit here, writing this book, in the tropical heat of

Cairns. But as we entered the room that night, Debbie was sitting up in her bed, pale-faced.

Debbie was nauseous and had a migraine. Classic symptoms of Acute Mountain Sickness (AMS). We got an oxygen saturation reading off her finger using an oximeter. The reading didn't look good. I knew exactly how she felt. The first time you experience AMS symptoms, it can be terrifying; not just for you, but those around you as well. Luckily, Saimon had plenty of experience. With my own history, we felt confident that we could cope with the situation.

The temperatures can drop as low as -17 degrees Celsius overnight in the Everest trekking region. Accommodation is usually in non-insulated rooms with thin walls and windows, and cement or dirt floors. It is only comfortable if you have the right sleeping bag and clothing. There are no real heating options. If a chill set in, you have to work really hard to warm up. Until the sun hits the valley, drinking hot water, eating hot food, and wearing down clothing, is your best option. You have to anticipate the freezing temperatures and prepare ahead; begin warming up before nightfall.

We assured Debbie, and Pierre, that she would be alright; gave her a dose of ibuprofen and Diamox, then dipped a flannel in boiled water to put over her head and face. We prayed and kept her company until she began to relax and feel a bit better. In the morning, she looked brighter but decided that she and Pierre wouldn't continue any higher. They would stay at that altitude for the next day, then return to Namche, and wait for Jess and me there.

As we were spending the day there, Saimon took Jess, Pierre, myself and two guides on an acclimatisation walk. Leaving Debbie at the guesthouse to sit in the sun and read, we began to climb a slope high above Dole. After some time, Jess decided to turn back. I walked further on, then rested. I wedged myself in against a rock that overlooked the mountain peaks across from me and the valley below. Pierre wanted to push on a bit further to experience a higher altitude.

As I rested, I sat in awe of the natural beauty. I began to cry as I worshipped God, the creator of all of this.

"This is the most beautiful thing I have ever seen!" I told Him.

"It's got nothing on me," He replied.

I remember deliberately noting my senses sitting there perched amid the Himalayas. I smelt the juniper crushed under my boots and seat. Felt the chilly breeze numb my nose and forehead. Heard the wind whoosh gently through the valley, and admired the icy snow that blanketed the peaks. The demonstration of God's creation was spectacular. But I also began to consider that even this incredible beauty and perfection in comparison—nothing surpasses Him in glory. It was right and fitting that I should hear those words, "It's got nothing on Me." Even now, I am thankful for that moment alone on the mountainside. Far away from my loved ones, but close to God.

In the sunshine, the next morning, we said our temporary goodbyes and the team split up. Bikash and a porter accompanied Debbie and Pierre downwards. Saimon and the other porters continued upwards with Jess and I, towards Machermo. Although it is always very emotional saying good-bye, it is important to stay focussed on what lay ahead. We set off with our faces turned towards Gokyo, making good time to Machermo, our last stop before the final village and the summit.

I am not sure when it happened, but I realised that I could visualise myself climbing up Gokyo Ri, the summit. I knew then that I had the strength to do it. Jess and I talked about how we would encourage each other anytime we were tempted to give up. I knew how much I needed positivity. I remembered how Saimon had spoken encouragement to me when Danny and I were nearing Annapurna Base Camp (ABC) years before. How I began to cry and almost stopped moving.

Saimon changed my focus and said, "You can do it, Aunty, yes you can. It is only a little further, you can do it."

I believed him, and I did it.

Although ABC is at a lower altitude than Gokyo Ri, it is challenging due to the climb you do over a couple of days. From that experience, I fully believe in the power of positivity to inspire others to push through when they don't know they can. Of course, there is a time to stop. And I have known that also. However, that was not now. Not yet.

Jess and I reached Gokyo Lake Village around 11am. I stated that if the sun was out, and we felt ok, we would go for the summit that afternoon. We had not been given the opportunity the year before as snowy weather prevented us from climbing. This year was going to be different. Most people rest and wait until the next morning to complete the final part of the trek. They rise early, hoping to catch a sunrise. But I wasn't risking that. I knew that anything could happen overnight. It had been six years and four attempts to reach Gokyo Ri. Jess and I both felt good, so we headed off at around 1:30pm.

It is a 500m climb in altitude to reach the Ri. When we had hiked upwards for around 1.5 hours, we asked Saimon how much further we had left. He said we were halfway. It was very discouraging. He never told us how long it would take, only that it wasn't far. He knew how slow I could walk when I got tired. But I kept my promise of maintaining positivity, and encouraged Jess along the way.

Jess stopped multiple times and asked, "How many more minutes?"

"Not far."

She never got the answer she wanted.

We kept going.

At some point, after about 2.5 hours, three trekkers came down the pathway towards us. They told us the good news. It was worth it. I had been looking at majestic views for over an hour and begun to silently doubt if it really could be much better at the top and should I really go through more pain to get there.

But they repeated, "It is worth it!"

I forced myself to believe them and pressed on with Jess slowly but surely just behind. After 3 hours we arrived. I could see the lakes far below almost covered in cloud and Gokyo like a tiny miniature village in the distance dwarfed by dozens of peaks, including Everest, on the horizon. At 5357m I felt like I was on top of the world! We laughed, and I cried. Each of us took a moment on the summit to give thanks, take photos, and just stand in silence. It seemed that we were all experiencing something special. We were higher than the clouds, overlooking the earth.

I had achieved my goal and shared the experience with someone.

It was Jess's first time in Nepal, and she had been able to reach Gokyo Ri. She could probably do much higher climbs if she was determined. So, while it was full credit to her ability, I believe that it was also partly to do with our teamwork and support that she could make it. Sometimes we break through a barrier, and we take others with us. I think that is what happened that day.

As does happen when you reach the top of a mountain, both literally and figuratively, you can't stay there. We had another 2.5 hours of walking to do, it was getting close to sunset, and we were tired. We quickly finished taking photos and began the walk down. The sun dipped behind the mountains while we walked with the light of our head torches, our legs quivering with tiredness through the dark, for the last 1.5 hours. When we finally reached the tea house, I could barely move. Bodily exhaustion, similar to after childbirth, absorbed me. Despite that, I knew that I had to eat and drink warm things. Our exhilaration from reaching the summit, now gone, we slouched on the benches, too tired to even sit upright.

In the early hours of the morning, I developed a terrible migraine and felt the familiar sensations of altitude sickness. I woke Jess up so that she could keep watch on me and pray. I took some Diamox, and some pain relief, and sat in bed, sipping hot water from my thermos. Praying for the morning. Experience taught me that I would be ok. The discomfort of nausea, headache, difficulty breathing, and fear slowly subsided as I thought about God and His great love for all the earth. The first rays of sunlight began to stream over the sacred Gokyo Lake. Whether poetically or prophetically, God's grace healed me through the sun's warmth. I felt well again. At that time, I meditated on my belief that Jesus is the son of God. That, through Jesus, He healed us all from our own brokenness and restored us to a right relationship with God the Father. I felt like I had just experienced that in a new and special way. I want to carry those moments in my heart for a long time.

Our reunion with Debbie and Pierre in Namche called for a celebration. We sat on bunks overlooking Thamserku peak, drank shots of Khukri rum (Nepali Rum), and sang *Freefallin* (Tom Petty) at the top of our lungs.

Moments that make the trip.

Moments that create lifetime memories.

Friends made then are lifers.

Chapter 14

Monkeys and Bananas

K athmandu was noisy and vibrant after having spent two weeks in the serenity of the mountains. Our trekking team had a few more days left to squeeze in as much of the city sights as they could. There was food to devour, drinks to enjoy, and shopping sprees that begged to fill suitcases with souvenirs. One thing I especially wanted to do was pierce my nose. I had considered it for a while, and it was as if the successful trek gave me the excuse, or courage, to go through with it. I faint very easily, and suspected that a new piercing would be just the occasion to warrant a good faint. I did my best to warn my friends and the piercer, but I don't think they were quite prepared for it.

The piercing and tattoo business operated in the centre of Thamel, a clean and tidy staircase led to the parlour. Cleanliness is always a good sign if you are about to have a procedure, whether medical or body art. The staff nodded when I explained that I may faint. Debbie, Pierre, and Jess accompanied me into the back room. Pierre was going to get a tattoo, and Jess had decided to get her nose pierced too. I lay back on the chair, and they got to work. I lasted about 1 minute. The needle was halfway through my nose cartilage; I swore loudly, then passed out cold.

I'm not sure how long I was out for, but by the time I came to, the nose stud was in, and Debbie was slapping my face and calling my name. I shyly apologised for my behaviour, and together we all had a bit of a laugh. After the other two went through their treatments, without incident, we all went for lunch. My nose was a little sore, but I loved the new look. My Nepali friends immediately commented on it, pointing and smiling; they seemed pleased that I was willing to participate in acts of cultural significance. Although not all women in Nepal have nose piercings, as it is not permitted for some ethnic groups, it is a very common site. I was happy to blend in a bit more now.

As a team, we had made Four Red Doors our home. Debbie and Pierre in apartment No. 4, Jess and I in No. 3. Although each apartment had it's own kitchen, we often shared meals around the long dining table and enjoyed morning devotions in my lounge. One morning we were all out of milk. Pierre, who was feeling familiar with the twisting, turning lanes, was keen to go buy our milk. There, on the corner, was a tiny window shop that opened every day for the basics like tea, sugar, eggs, and milk. Pierre was also eager to use some Nepali. We had a quick lesson.

"So how do you ask for milk?"

"*Dudh chha?*"

"Duude chaaa?"

"*Dudh chha?*"

Pierre disappeared down the steps, reciting his newly learnt phrase. Not long after, he returned frowning, but with two small packets of milk. He quickly accused me of teaching him something rude in Nepali, claiming that the shopkeeper was offended by the question. We all had a good laugh about it as we made coffee. Pierre maintains that it was not his pronunciation, rather my teaching. I'm quite sure that the shopkeeper is well used to foreigners getting it wrong.

A week later, as my Thai Airways flight left the tarmac, I watched through the window as the buildings of Kathmandu became small dots. As the plane rose higher, the clouds suddenly separated the city and me. I knew that it would only be a matter of weeks, and I would return with my family. It is always easier leaving when you know that you will be back.

Once again, Danny was waiting for me back in Australia. This time I met him in Sydney. I excitedly told him everything about my successful trek, and he commented on my new nose piercing. We spent the next few days exploring the beautiful bays around Sydney Harbour, walking for hours at a time. Danny had always been much fitter than I, but for once, I had an advantage. I was experiencing the bonus of extra blood cells as a result of my trek and acclimatisation. I found that I could race up the steep steps in Potts Point two at a time while Danny slowly climbed behind me. I laughed at him as he plodded along. I enjoyed my short-lived advantage, and within three weeks, all was back to normal. My athletic prowess is not much to rave about.

We returned to Cairns, and it wasn't long before Nepal was front and centre again in our plans. Our eldest daughter, Jessica, her husband Adrian, and their three children—Jacob, Beau, and Joseph —were booked to fly to Kathmandu in early December and begin their one-month volunteer program with INA, then meet us in January to trek. I was so excited for them, knowing how much they would love it. Having been in Nepal with us 18 months earlier, Jacob took the role of the group guide. He happily explained what would happen when they arrived in Kathmandu, and all about the monkeys, how to say *namaste*, and the yummy food. His two younger brothers absorbed every word but found it hard to imagine this new country with another language and cold, snowy peaks. We waved goodbye to them as they turned around for the last time before disappearing through the immigration doors at the Cairns International Airport. I couldn't wait to hear from them once they landed and experienced their first impression of Nepal.

Meanwhile, in Australia, Christmas came and went. It grew hotter and wetter. We spoke many times to the grandsons over the internet. We enjoyed seeing photos of goats, the hospital compound, and Jessica holding twins she helped to deliver. We heard stories of staff devotions and prayer in the hospital, and how all three grandsons were trying to speak Nepali with the local children. Adrian spent several days a week in theatre and emergency while Jessica worked the other 4 days in midwifery. She also had the opportunity to do some professional development with the hospital staff and trek to a nearby village to participate in an outreach clinic. In one month, they were able to be a part of so many new experiences. Some of the less wonderful ones included: many cold showers; a basic diet and menu options; living with three boys in a single room arrangement, and stretching their cross-cultural practices to the maximum. By the end of the month, they looked forward to experiencing the big city life and tourist activities of Kathmandu.

January is cold in Nepal. Our flight landed, and Lama met us at the exit area in a new taxi this time. We wondered where the old Suzuki was, and Lama explained that he now rented a taxi. This was one of the new regulations as Nepal attempted to reduce the number of old vehicles in the city area. We settled into the car seats, and I did my usual greeting to Nepal. I made it a custom to roll down the taxi window, stick my head out and yell, "Kathmandu!" every time I arrived back in the country. Motorcyclists and pedestrians stared and smiled as I happily waved to them. It was good to be back again, so soon after my departure.

Danny and I returned to the familiar top floor of Four Red Doors and turned on the gas heater. I checked for hot water in the shower, then we unpacked our things; this would be home for the next 10 days. The gas heater was a new development for us. It felt luxurious to be able to heat up our living space. The hot water was warm enough, so we showered and got ready for our walk into Thamel. The first walk down the streets can take hours. Not only because it is interesting, but because so many of our long-term friends work in those streets. It is always fun to see their smiling faces and hear their "namaste," as they seemingly appear from nowhere. Danny is very social when he is travelling. I always tease him that our friends in Nepal love Danny more than me. I don't mind if it is true. Danny is a very kind, generous and sometimes cheeky guy. He seems to know how to joke with the Nepali men, and despite cultural and language barriers, it works. I put this down to Danny's easy and friendly love for all people. I believe this is a gift from God. I often watch and learn from him.

Included in our visits and *namastes,* we see Dipak in the Dolphin Guesthouse. Dipak had looked after us at the guesthouse since we first visited Nepal. But now, he and another couple of men had recently taken over ownership of the guesthouse. Dipak was standing on the front steps as we had seen him do over the last 8 years. He shyly greeted us and invited us into the same quiet cool foyer that we first experienced on my original trip to Nepal. The same chairs and travel books on the shelf. The same faded map of Nepal on the wall. Only the staff had changed a little and the view from the rooftop. The new hotel behind the guesthouse, now complete, blocked the mountains from view even on a clear day. We enquired how business was going, and after some teasing about getting a wife, we continued on our way. We knew we had plenty of tea to drink in many shops along the street.

As I have written, I often wondered if my Nepali friends only like me for what I can give. Likewise, I wondered if my relationships with our many shopkeeper friends would remain if we never did any business with them. But that is a useless debate. Many of them have had no business from me for years and still welcome me in for a chat and tea. I believe that their warm and open hearts are genuine. I believe that if I ever needed assistance, they would be there for me. They would step in for me no matter what.

Two years earlier in Nepal there was one occasion when I could not return from Nawalparasi due to landslides. I was desperate to return to Kathmandu the next day, as I had already overstayed my schedule with a local family. They were extremely hospitable, but I really needed to get back to some western food, bedding, and my own space. But the biggest challenge had been the language. It was the first time in my life that I had spent an entire 8 days speaking mainly Nepali, and only some basic English. I was exhausted. The family tried to find a way to send me back by plane, but I really don't think they had the power to make a booking. They certainly did not have the money for it.

I called on a favour. I was learning that this is what you do in Nepal. I phoned Saimon and asked him to source me a seat out of Chitwan airport, and I would pay for it when I got back to Kathmandu. Basically, he had to give his word to one of his contacts, in the airlines, that this woman from Australia would be good for the money. The flight was booked. After 45 minutes in a Tuk Tuk, and a short domestic flight back to Kathmandu, I had experienced the value of connection in a new way. It really is who you know that matters.

After spending time with friends, enjoying Chicken Chilli, Dahl bat, Ghorka beer, and trying to catch a glimpse of the Himalayas from the rooftop; it was now time for our family to arrive. We organised Lama and his brother-in-law to bring two taxis to the domestic airport at around 7:30pm so we could meet their 8pm flight from Rukum. In true Nepali style time, around 9pm, the plane landed - just an hour late. After a short bus ride around the tarmac for several minutes, our family tumbled through the doors. Jessica looked so beautiful, brightly adorned with shawl and *kurtha suruwal*. The children were excited, all gushing to speak at once. Adrian, clearly the organised one, searched for the luggage area and practised his perfect namaste on Lama. We took photos and kissed and hugged around twenty times.

Back at the apartment, I had prepared supper. Jessica had already told me how after the month in Rukum, she longed for cheese, bread, wine, and chocolates. I had sourced all four from the Lazimpat shops, which were stocked to supply and satisfy the tastebuds of the expats living in the area. We feasted on the goodies, gave everyone a warm shower and put them to bed. I think they must have felt that they had arrived in luxury after their much smaller residence in the hospital compound.

It was totally wonderful being able to share my beautiful Nepal with our family. They also had plenty to share about their month in the village. We immediately switched into tourist mode—exploring the sights of Kathmandu: Swayambhunath Stupor, Durbar Squares, Asan Bazaar, New Road, Thamel, and meeting all our friends. Travelling in Nepal with three boys, aged 9, 7, and 5, was exciting and exhausting. Our Nepali friends loved the grandsons and found them very entertaining.

One of the boys' favourite meeting places was in our friend, Khanal's, pashmina shop. If anyone was ever lost, or our group split up and needed to arrange a meeting place, it was at Khanal's shop. If we were taking too long in another shop selecting jewellery or getting that last bit of trekking gear, my grandsons could always be found sitting at the colourful little desk. Sipping milky tea and giggling about something with Khanal and his delightfully friendly shop assistant, Bunni. Many hours were spent wiping up spilt tea and experimenting with newly learnt Nepali words.

One of the other activities that my family enjoyed in Kathmandu, was watching monkeys. Our apartment block is quite close to the Indian Embassy. The embassy is also adjacent to a parkland that hosts dozens of monkey families. Although there are walls around the embassy, this doesn't stop monkeys.

From the rooftop of Four Red Doors, you can spot the monkeys cheekily climbing tree trunks, and balancing along electrical wiring. Springing from one building to the next, the monkeys made their way around the embassy compound or across to the nearby homes. One afternoon, Adrian, Jessica, Danny, and I were enjoying a glass of wine and some snacks on the roof, we spotted two monkeys squatting on the windowsill of the neighbouring hotel block. They watched us as we chatted and ate. Adrian went downstairs and got some bananas to entice the monkeys to come closer, thinking that it would be a fun thing to do.

Suddenly, faster than we had imagined, the biggest monkey sprang over to our building and ran along the edge of the balcony towards the bananas. Jessica and Adrian jumped back towards the steps, and I retreated to the far side of the rooftop. The monkey came within half a metre of us, hissing and growling through gritted teeth. He wasn't going to back down over a banana. We were terrified. Having not expected such an aggressive response. We had thought it would be a mild and fun experience.

Eventually, using a chair as an intimidation method, the monkey retreated to the hotel next door. We were stunned. Laughing hysterically from fear, we vowed not to play with those monkeys again. A few weeks later, after our trek, I was sitting near the open window of the ground floor flat when an aggressive monkey ran towards the window and attempted to get in. Fortunately, metal bars blocked its access. But it didn't stop me from screaming as I sat face to face with a monkey's mouth full of sharp, growling teeth.

Apart from exploring Kathmandu with the family, one of the other main reasons we had returned that January was to go trekking together. Adrian and Danny planned to go to Everest Base Camp. Jessica and I would stay with the boys in Namche, then descend and return to Kathmandu to wait for the guys. After a few more days of traipsing around Kathmandu, showing off all my favourite spots, Saimon arrived to meet us in the city. We began to finalise our plans for the trek.

Once again, I picked up my pack, put it on the bed, and began the ritual of repacking the gear. It only seemed like a day or two since I had done the same thing in preparation for trekking with Debbie, Pierre, and Jess Earl. Yet, it had been nine weeks. The methodical process of ensuring everything was in the right pocket, zip, and clip began again. It is not a happy thing to find that halfway through the trek, that packet of wipes you really need has gone astray. Over the years, Danny and I have created a system for where certain items were packed and carried on our treks. I'm sure everyone does this. But the situation of trekking with three young boys made the process even more important.

Saimon stayed with us the night before the trek. Sleeping on the narrow couch beneath the window where the monkey had climbed through years before. At around 4:30am, the alarms woke us from our snuggly beds to brush our teeth and drink tea. We somehow managed to gather all our backpacks, duffle bags, trekking poles, water bottles, five adults, and three children into the two taxis waiting in the dark laneway close to the apartments. At the airport, we tripped and tumbled out of the taxis. Refusing the usual offers of random people to carry our luggage, we all made our way towards the terminal. Except, we were so organised that we arrived before the doors were even open. We had to wait outside for around 20 minutes, supervising eager and excited children and keeping our place in the line; always a challenge in Nepal.

We were on our way to the mountains again!

Chapter 15

Trekking is like life

One of the joys of trekking in Nepal is the fun you have with the porters. We were accompanied by a couple of the same porters we had trekked with before over the last several years. Bikkash, acting as the assistant guide and porter; Rum, smiley and helpful; and Prabesh, quiet but strong and dependable. The grandsons loved having their help, especially when it came to our youngest. Joseph was just 5 years old, although full of energy and enthusiasm, he sometimes needed assistance on the bigger steps.

The trekking trail to Namche is a well-worn track. You could easily do it without a guide or porters. But we love investing in the lives of the young men who come along with us. We get to talk about their families, learn about their home village, culture, and what dreams they have for the future. We also get to share our faith in a way that is, hopefully, relatable. I consider that if God has sent me to love the people of Nepal, then I can share that love in any way, and at any opportunity, I am able to.

Ever since 2012, when we began trekking in Nepal, I have had the honour of leading our groups in prayer at the start of every trek. We usually do it on the morning that we set off from Phak Ding, after our first night in the mountains. It was always freezing, with everyone rugged up in their jackets and scarves. We take a group photo out the front of the same guest lodge every time. Then we gather around, holding each other's gloved hands, and I pray the blessing over our group. Regardless of what personal beliefs the trekking team members had, this ritual connected us in a common act. The prayer wasn't a responsibility attributed to my role as group leader, nor a simple act of faith. It was an encouragement that we were not alone as we trekked through the isolated mountain trails.

I am aware that mountain culture in Nepal acknowledges that the gods have authority in the mountains. So, I hope that my prayer resonated with them and showed respect for the country, the mountains, the people, and the spiritual sense of place. This was my prayer:

God, you go before us in the journey. We ask that you guide us, give us the wisdom, strength, and grace to complete the trek. Help us to see you in the mountains and the trees and the animals. Help us to work with each other. We ask you for safety for each of us and that your will would be done for our team. Bless us, we ask in the name of your son Jesus Christ,

Amen.

With the first night, and blessing under our belts, we headed toward Namche. The weather was cool and dry. Because I had just been on the trail nine weeks earlier, I had a strong sense of deja vu. Danny and Jacob had been there two years earlier, but for Jessica, Adrian, Beau, and Joseph; it was all new. Mule bells rang out across the valley. Dust floated, kicked up by passing trekkers, and settled on the tops of our boots; coating the rocks that haphazardly created the pathway. As always, the hike to Namche was long and strenuous. Often a huge shock for those who consider themselves reasonably fit back home at sea level. *Breath in, breath out, walk to the rhythm of your breath. As I breathe, then I can move*, I thought, coaching myself internally.

Our family and porters pushed on, each of us settling into our own pace. As the day wore on, our helpful porters alternately carried the day packs as needed, and the children began to drag their feet. There is a small village just before Namche. It is a false hope for the newcomer. I have been tricked many times before, so this time, I don't change my pace. I don't surrender my will power. Ahead of us remains a slow push. Up stone steps, up around the final corner, then there it is— Namche Bazar: the iconic trekking village!

In earlier years, we thought we needed to have cash for the whole trek. That always meant carrying thousands of rupees in wads of notes, stuffed into secret pockets in backpacks and passport holders. But over the years, ATMs have popped up more often, and many shopkeepers in Namche and Kathmandu will let you use your Visa card for the more expensive purchases. However, cash remains preferred and is still what we continue to carry with us. We also developed a habit of carrying some US dollars in case we spend all our rupee. Members of our trekking teams have often shopped for last minute gear, extra snacks, and gifts in Namche. The streets are filled with little shops and doorways that you need to duck through. Yaks wandered around the paved corners, and cafés sold everything from margarita pizza to black forest gateau.

Once we all finally arrived in Namche, we celebrated with the usual photos and hugs. It is a great effort for anyone, and especially for our young grandsons. However, the pause was short-lived as our hotel stood at the top of the village, which meant another 15 minutes of climbing steps until we could really rest. The Hotel Tibet has looked after us during every trek over the last 7 years and it feels like home in the mountains.

We always choose rooms that get the afternoon sun. The windowsill is covered in a varnished ply, and the glass panes keep out the wind but let in the warmth. My favourite room is at the end of the hallway as it has two windows and twice the warmth. If I can, I grab the bed under the window and use the whole sill as my bench space. Anyone who has trekked in Nepal, would know what a luxury it is to have a bench or windowsill in your room. Often you are provided with a bed only and nowhere to place your belongings off the floor. Hotel Tibet is like a 5-star hotel when it comes to these matters!

Our family settled into their rooms. We booked three rooms—one for the three grandsons, and one room each for the adult couples. When it comes to leading a group, I have noticed that most people need a little time out during the first afternoon you arrive in Namche. Time to have a warm drink, unpack a bit, fluff up their sleeping bags, and have a snooze in the sun rays that beam in and give you that dozy, somewhat drunken feeling you get from an afternoon nap. It quickly turns cold as the sun dips behind the mountain. Then the dining room beckons with more hot drinks and games of UNO.

It sounds idyllic. And very 'civilised' as Danny would say. If you didn't venture any further in altitude and enjoyed the surrounding day walks and views, you would still experience a fantastic trek. There would be no danger to your health regarding altitude sickness. You could access a pharmacy if needed and could get a helicopter evacuation in an emergency. There are plenty of food and drink options, warm rooms, the potential of having a hot shower, shops, yaks, incredible views, and plenty of other trekkers and locals to meet. But it is the gateway to the rest of the trekking areas. From there you reach,

Gokyo, the three passes, and the iconic Everest Base Camp (EBC).

It was to EBC that Danny and Adrian were planning to go. But the day after we arrived in Namche, our acclimatisation day, and we walked up to the highest hotel in the world, the Everest View Hotel, someone in our team began to have doubts.

It wasn't until late that afternoon when we were all in a café where you can play board games like Battleships and Chess while enjoying a snack and beverage. Adrian said that he was having second thoughts. It wasn't actually clear to me why he didn't want to go. But I had heard and felt those things before from others in my groups. And in my own heart and mind. You see, once you get to Namche, you feel safe and warm. You begin to ask yourself; can it be any better if I go up higher? You realise that, despite your manageable comfort level here, you are uncertain how bad it may get if you continue. Your head may feel a bit fuzzy, and you puff a lot more when you walk up the steps and exert any effort. These things raise doubt.

What if it is so cold that I totally hate it?

What if I get sick and can't get help?

What if I can't make it and it is a waste of my efforts?

Will I fail?

On and on, the self-doubt can go if left unchecked.

From experience and how much it challenged me, I have found it is like going into childbirth for your second or third time. I know what is ahead. That in itself is scary. The flip side is that I can use my experience and what I know to increase my chances of success this time; not only for myself but for others.

So, we listened to Adrian. Then I pulled out my Group Leader voice and explained some things. "It's not unusual to be uncertain at this point. Often, for no particular reason, a person will wish to just stay put in Namche. The unknown beyond is a real mental challenge. And combined with the culture, food, cold, and everything, it is tempting to settle for what is easier. But tomorrow, when you wake up and see the sun is out, snow sparkling on the mountain, and others preparing to go onwards, you will feel inspired. Your courage and decisiveness will return. You are in good hands with your team, and Danny will be with you. Allow your doubts to exist but decide on what you will later regret if you do not give it a go."

It's important to now say that it probably wasn't just my words that had an impact. Jessica then took the chance to tell Adrian what she thought about it. She proceeded to inform him that if he didn't accompany her dad and give the trek a go, she would step into that role.

"If you don't go, and I go instead and make it to EBC, you will have to hear about it for the rest of your life!" She stated.

Now, I am unsure what it was exactly that turned Adrian from uncertainty to a decision to give it go. But that decision was entirely up to him and somehow, he found the strength and willpower to commit. This was the plan: he and Danny would rise early the next morning with another young trekker named Perry, who we had met on the first day of the trail, and embark on the next stage of the trek. Jessica, the children, and

I would walk with them for the first few hours, then hug them goodbye as they turned the corner towards Tengboche and the EBC trail. And that is exactly what happened.

During the time we waited in Namche, we watched yaks, searched for snow, and played UNO in the warm dining room, sometimes with a grey cat on our laps. I also had a small job to do. Three years earlier, when our son Daniel and his girlfriend Breanna were with us in Namche, I had taken a photo of a couple of women warming themselves by a small fire. We had laughed at my awkward attempts to speak Nepali. That photo had become a poster that I used at community and fundraising events for WWP. Beneath the smiling photo of the women were the words:

She did what she could.

Taken directly from the book of Mark, chapter 14. They were the words of Jesus, spoken to a woman in one of the local religious leaders' home. Although unnamed, she is famous for her brash, improper act of anointing Jesus with a perfumed oil that held the value of a year's wages. Her act of lavish love, amid her own uncertain life, has been recorded and retold over hundreds of generations as an example to us all. What she did mattered to Jesus. What we do matters also.

Over the years, we had used and re-used that poster as part of our story. I even had a copy of it on the back of my bathroom door. It was a daily reminder of the opportunity and responsibility I have to do something meaningful with my life.

Before we left Cairns in early January, preparing to fly to Nepal and meet our family, Danny had an idea. He suggested that I make extra copies of the poster, and while I was in Namche, try to find the main woman in the photo to give her a copy. It was now time to find that woman.

My first response was to go to the street, where I remembered seeing her those years earlier. I asked around, and someone sent me to a small shop a little higher in the village. After showing the poster to the shopkeeper, her eyes lit up as she laughed. Yes, she knew who it was. Excitedly she led me to the end of the laneway and up three steps into a dim tea room attached to a tiny kitchen area where a woman stood boiling water for the tea. Immediately I could see it was the woman in the photo. After a few exchanges in Nepali, she called in her brother-in-law, who helped with a little English translation. It was wonderful. She laughed and giggled as she looked at the picture. I asked her if I could put up the poster and take a picture of her next to it.

"*Ek chin*," she replied and disappeared out the back somewhere.

She returned with a blue jacket and her jewellery. She had gone to change into the same clothes she had worn in the original photo. She hurried to put up the poster. It was a little crooked and stuck in the middle of a wall which seemed strange to me. But she beamed as she stood beneath it. We took photos, then she insisted that she make me tea. I hung around with her for a while longer, but it was getting late and cold by then. Eventually, I explained that my daughter would be waiting for me, and I said goodbye. I don't know if she ever really understood why I had a poster of her. Still, she seemed proud to have a copy of it on her wall for all her customers and family to see. I wonder if I returned, would she still have it hung there?

A few days later, we arrived back in cold Kathmandu. It was the usual January weather; chilly, dim, and dusty. We were all tired, and our grandsons were testing us. We moved into the ground floor apartment of Four Red Doors, just for that week, and tried to settle into a routine with the children. With Danny and Adrian still somewhere in the mountains, Jessica and I took care of the three boys. We found it challenging. For some reason, Joseph was behaving out of character. He would cry, scream, run around, laugh and generally be awful. We finally realised it was a mixture of too much sugar in the Nepali tea and absolute exhaustion from the trek. We quickly revised our menus and bed times.

Just as we solved one problem, another arose. It was early evening, and we were organising dinner and showers. Beau, the middle son, began clutching his abdomen and moaning in agony. He lay on the couches in the living room, near the heater. I tried to help him by giving him a warm cloth for his stomach and telling him to lie on his side. But it worsened, over an hour or so, and it became clear that we couldn't leave him in that condition. I was actually a little afraid. What if it was appendicitis? He had complained about some pain, on and off, over the last few days of the trek

I had been to Nepal 10 times and thankfully had not needed a doctor until then. But by Beau's behaviour, we had to do something. I actually didn't really know which hospital would be good for a child. I prayed for help with this and called our landlord, Urmila. She promptly told me that a children's hospital was 5 minutes taxi ride away and that we should go there for good care.

While Jessica prepared a small bag with food, water, blankets, passports and money, I raced down the alley, around the three corners and onto Lazimpat Road to hail a taxi. The driver came quickly, and Jessica managed to half carry Beau into the vehicle. I negotiated the fare with the driver and pressed him on.

"Chhito chhito jaanus! (Go fast please!)".

While cleaning up the remains of our noodle dinner, I prayed for the doctors to have wisdom. Within the hour, I was surprised to hear Jessica and Beau knocking on the door. Jessica explained that they had seen a doctor immediately; he had prescribed antibiotics and an oral drink for a bladder infection. Beau was a lot calmer and ready for bed now. Thank you, Lord! We all hugged Beau several times and gave thanks. Everyone went to bed happy.

Adrian and Danny arrived back in Kathmandu several days later, having happily and safely reached EBC. They had incredible weather, walking through deep snow and white-out weather to accomplish their goal. Although both of them experienced some fairly challenging altitude sickness symptoms, they managed it with some pain relief, rest, and warm food to help with the migraines.

We celebrated by going to eat at our favourite restaurant, OR2K. Together we sat around the low tables on the floor and devoured pasta, naan bread, tasty salads, hummus, and Ghorka beer. There was a good vibe all around us. Other customers laughed and chatted. It seemed that everyone was happy. It is the type of place where you take off your shoes, find a cushion, sit down, order a drink, and talk about your adventures together. Danny and Adrian filled us in with their stories of deep snow, a birthday cake cooked in Lobuche at 4940m, photoshoots in their underwear at EBC, and a sick porter who had to return to a lower altitude. As was the case when Jess and I climbed up to Gokyo Ri months earlier, Adrian and Danny completed their trek with success. And while many trekkers don't make it to their planned destination, it is so awesome when you do. Both experiences are valuable. We learn when we have to deal with disappointment, and we use those lessons to assist us with the next attempt. Trekking at altitude is so much like life.

Then it was our turn. Jessica and I shared our stories of slow scenic walks around Namche, goat spotting in the hills, and finishing our trek in gentle falling snow on the way back to Lukla. Then we moved to the challenges. Being stuck in the freezing Lukla airport for 6 hours with three tired and annoyingly behaved children. We told of being bumped from our flights because we didn't seem to have a powerful person advocating for us. We talked about Joseph's sugar overdose and how Beau got sick. Even though the stories about the children may seem challenging, and actually it was; it was such a buzz to think that they had trekked in the Himalayas and that we got to share it with them.

Eventually, our month together in Nepal came to a close. We were all booked to depart on the same afternoon. The night before we left, Saimon and his wife, Sumjana, came to say goodbye. They were in Kathmandu for some medical appointments and made their way across town for one last meal together. After dinner, they gave each of us a khada—a scarf of farewell and respect. We hugged and took photos. The children had grown fond of Saimon and he of them. Then they walked out the door and around the corner, disappearing into the dark alley. Jacob cried. It was a sad goodbye. Saimon had been our guide for 7 years, and his family had become like family to ours.

The next morning, Lama and his brother drove us to the airport. I was glad that we were all leaving at the same time. I remembered how much I had missed our other family members, Daniel and Breanna, when they left us in Nepal. I didn't want to feel that again. Once in the gate lounge at Tribhuvan Airport, it always seems like forever to wait until the flight is actually ready to depart. As if there is bound to be a delay. But then, in the manner that we had grown accustomed to, there was a huge rush. Suddenly, everyone was herded onto a transit bus and dropped off at the aircraft a few metres away. The friendly Thai Airways staff welcomed us. We settled into the short flight to Bangkok, watching as the Himalayas spread out beneath the wings of the aircraft.

Immoveable and ancient.

Chapter 16

All other streams are dry

A lot happened during 2019.

We moved twice. Firstly, into Danny's parents' home, for a brief month or two until our house was available. Then we moved again, back into our home. The home that we had built ourselves years before. The home where we raised our kids; growing as adults alongside them. For the past five years, our daughter Jessica and her family rented our home so they could study and start their healthcare careers. When they received jobs out of town, it was time for them to move out and for us to move back in. During those 5 years, we lived in a great little one-bedroom unit, occupying one half of a shed. It was extremely comfortable, practical, and stylish; easy to keep organised. Moving back into our larger home would mean a lot more work. But it also meant we could host a social gathering larger than 2 people, and our family could stay with us when they visited. We also paid off our house that year. It was a strange feeling. When you have been working towards something for so long, it is great to finish it. But, also a bit surreal. Sometimes I even forgot and would try to include those payments in the budget again. I didn't do that for long. It was great to have more freedom to decide what to do with our income.

Our son also got married that year, several weeks after we moved back home. It was a beautiful wedding, and we love his wife, Breanna. The third nurse in the family! There were a lot of great things that happened that year.

Yet, I felt low. Extremely low. I couldn't put my finger on it. I had been doing a few night shifts at work, and that often played with my emotions. But perhaps it wasn't just me. Perhaps it was those around me also. Perhaps it was an opportunity for something to change. Perhaps it was because it was a change of season, ready to welcome something new. Or, perhaps, to farewell something old. Whatever it was, I wasn't feeling very hopeful.

One day, I was sitting outside in the garden with my Bible and notebook, desperate for God to speak to me. I began to read the story of the woman at the well. Jesus and the woman began to speak together, then Jesus asked her to draw him some water to drink. Something which was considered unusual in that setting and culture. Eventually, the conversation turned; the woman asked Jesus for the water he offers—the water of eternal life.

YOU CAN'T RIDE A YAK

"Sir, give me this water, so that I won't
get thirsty and have to keep coming
here every day to draw water."

(John 4:15)

I sat under a little bush, contemplating what I had read. I watched the birds and listened to the distant sound of traffic. Turning my attention away from the birds, I looked out over the view of cane fields.

"If you really are the living water, and I have already received you, why do I keep getting thirsty all over again?" I asked God, bluntly.

Gently, but very clearly, I sensed Him explain, "Because you don't stay at my well. You wander off and try other things to satisfy yourself."

At that moment, the conversation with God continued.

A conversation that sparked a new desire. A desire to seek God as my only source of comfort, peace, joy, and all other positive feelings I lack at any time.

"God, I want to find you as my true source of happiness, fulfilment, and peace. I am tired of filling up my lack with my own solutions. Even though at times I have sought you, I also follow other paths which have eventually only led me to dryness and thirst. Help me and remind me what you are teaching me here today."

A few days later, I found an old hymn, and it became a theme for me throughout the year. Although it was written around 200 years earlier, it was still relevant to me now.

> *Whom have we, Lord, but Thee,*
> *Soul thirst to satisfy?*
> *Exhaustless spring! The waters free!*
> *All other streams are dry.*

Mary Bowley (1813-1856)

My year began to change. I began to feel stronger and lighter. More focussed, knowing what I needed to be doing and how to get it done. But the biggest difference was in how I felt, and for that, I am grateful. Some of the reasons that I had felt so bad earlier in the year were known. Some reasons may have come from past choices in situations that arose at a time when I was most vulnerable and under pressure. I'm not all that sure, but one thing I do believe is that the water Jesus offered to the woman at the well, in John chapter 24, is the Holy Spirit—the water of life. He promised to be in me; filling me to overflow into others. Promising to quench my thirst and continue to do so as I drink from Him alone.

As I write this chapter, I am reminded of how difficult it was to realise that I needed to seek my every emotional and spiritual supply from God. I never want to have to go through that process again. I sought many other things. Some knowingly and others not so consciously. But I know it now. I also know why I really needed to learn that in 2019. There were so many things ahead.

To finish off the year, three things were planned. Two involved preaching, and the other exciting one was welcoming a new grandson. First, I needed to prepare for four weeks of preaching to around 19 different groups of women throughout South Australia, then after in Nepal. I serve with an organisation called Christian Women Communicating International (CWCI). In September, my job was to be the speaker in CWCI's ministry called 'Safari.' Safari is a way for CWCI to encourage Australian women living in remote and rural regions through the teaching and sharing of God's Word. Over the years, I have completed 3 Queensland Safaris, and 2 National Safaris. Every time I find it extremely challenging.

Why is it so challenging, since I do love preaching? I love sharing stories to encourage and challenge people to find and fulfil God's will for their lives. And while I do love it – it involves work and preparation. Prayer is certainly part of that preparation process. Honestly, one of the most challenging aspect is the actual practical elements of travel and having to work with complete strangers. Every time I participated in Safari; I spent those two weeks with another woman I had never met before. Yet, we must pray together, minister together, often share a room together, and have little time to be alone. the other challenge is that we have no idea how many women will meet with us, in each new town, and listen to us speak. Every place is different.

Some people are warm and happy to see me and lap up everything I have brought. Other times, there is weariness in the eyes of those who meet me. As if many years of religious duty has dampened the fire of their love for Christ and His work. It is very special to share time with those suffering apparent disheartenment or brokenness. It can be hard to minister in those situations, but every woman is important. I believe that God has chosen me to go. So, I must believe that every life I pray for, speak to, or share a coffee with, was intended to meet me for a divine reason. I have found, over the years, that the Safari ministry is such an unknown. Yet I do know that there will be an outcome from every act of love and prayer. Therefore, I remind myself that if God has called me, then I will go to love and serve. I then leave the rest to Him. I also marvel at the way God has used my work with CWCI to prepare me for Nepal. The uncomfortable, unpredictable nature of ministry on the road equips me for those same challenges in Nepal. I got tougher, but at the same time, softer. Softer to people's needs and to God's whispers.

I completed two weeks in South Australia; travelling from Adelaide to Cooper Pedy and through the country regions of the state. During that time, I was hosted by so many open-hearted and generous women. Many of them shared their struggles with me, and we prayed together for change, hope, and peace. They made me think of the women in Nepal, who I would soon be teaching and praying with. And although at times there was dryness in the land, dryness in the people I met, and even dryness in my own heart, I took time daily to drink from the refreshing water of Christ. I thought of Him, talked to Him, sang to Him, and listened to Him. And I found that stream to always run with fresh water.

Carole, one of my close friends and a very thorough Bible teacher, was going to join me in Nepal and assist me with the teaching at various conferences. We had a few weeks of uncertainty and changed plans due to some persecution of Christian foreigners in Nepal, but eventually, our dates were set. We planned and prayed. Then reminded ourselves that plans are ok, but prayer is better. Our theme for the conferences was to be: Wise Woman. We based our teachings on Proverbs 31 – A Woman of Influence.

Carole was ready to go. I still needed to complete a few things. Immediately after the two weeks in South Australia, I returned home for two days to finish an assignment for university. At the time, I was completing a course with Deakin University in International and Community Development. Then I flew to Sydney and spent two days with Danny before heading off to Nepal. Waiting for Carole and I were four women's conferences in four different parts of the Kathmandu Valley. There was a lot of work to do, and I was eager to arrive and get settled in before the busy 11-day schedule. But things didn't go quite as I would have liked.

As I have explained before, I fly standby on staff tickets. It is great because it saves me a lot of money and means I can travel to and from Nepal as often as I can fit it into my calendar. This time, I had a standby ticket booked; Sydney to Bangkok, then onto Kathmandu the following day. But when I was due to depart Sydney, the flight was full; no staff could get seats. So, I headed back to the hotel where Danny was staying for his work. I spent another day praying and preparing my messages. It seemed as if God had me there so that I could spend more time preparing, so I made the most of it.

The next day, I got a seat to Bangkok. But at the luggage claim, I did a thing you hope you never do. I mistakenly picked up someone else's suitcase. As soon as I went to open it in my hotel room, I knew. I ran like a desperate woman to the reception. I literally begged them to make a call for me to find out if my suitcase had been returned to the airport. Or worse, if my luggage was on its way to Europe or elsewhere. And I was praying. I did have all of my notes for my messages, sermon outlines, and itinerary, as I had packed the important documents in my carry-on bag. But all of my Nepali outfits, and other special things, were in my suitcase. It is difficult to source underwear and shoes in Nepal, as sizes can be tricky for westerners.

The hotel van drove me back to the airport, and I found the lost luggage office in the bowels of Bangkok Airport. I will say that although I was panicking inside, the staff were really helpful. I remember that at the baggage carousel, I had seen a woman from my flight looking at the bag that I collected. But she had walked away from it, so I assumed it was mine. Unfortunately, her bag and mine were identical, large green suitcases. I prayed that they were not on their way to another flight. Hoping that they, like me, had gone to their hotel and made the discovery before leaving the country.

The staff instructed me to go back to my hotel and wait for them to contact me. I sat down in the hotel's restaurant and tried to eat some food. Then I called Danny. He talked to some of his friends at Qantas, hoping to assist me from his side. It wasn't long before he called back and said they had found the owner of the bag that I had mistakenly collected. Then, at around 9pm that night, I received an email from the lost luggage staff explaining that my suitcase had been located, and someone would drop it off to the hotel at around 2am. The other passenger had returned it just as I had left the airport. She had only been staying in Bangkok for a few more hours, as she was on her way to Germany. Had she not gone to access the contents of her suitcase, and simply transited to another flight, it would have been goodbye to my belongings.

Now, with the suitcase back in my hands, I tried to get my flight out of Bangkok. For the next three days, I tried. Every day all the flights were full. I tried booking with other airlines; even that was impossible. I was prepared to pay whatever price. I spent hours at the airport every day, waiting for flights and trying to get an internet connection to search for other available flights. I booked and rebooked seats. My blood pressure felt like it was creeping up for the first time in my life. Every day that I didn't get a seat out of Thailand, I had to find somewhere else to stay for another night. Then rinse and repeat the whole process again the following day.

Earlier in the year I had dreamt about going to Asia. I dreamt that I was listening to a prophetic guest speaker at a conference. He was addressing the congregation at the close of his message. All the participants gathered around the front of the stage; I was among them.

"This year is the year for women to go and minister in… Asia!" The speaker prophesied.

I jumped up and began to yell in excitement.

When I had awoken, I knew that the dream prophecy was meant for me. I took it as a message from God. It was that dream that I needed to remember while I sat in Bangkok Airport day after day. God wanted me to minister in Asia – and for me, that meant Nepal. That year. So, I kept believing. And I kept looking for flights.

People in both Nepal and Australia prayed for me. Carole was due to arrive in Kathmandu, and I was meant to meet her at the airport. The conferences were scheduled to start the day after; we had no plan B. I had to get there. Miraculously, I found one seat on a China Eastern Airline flight to a city called Kunming; a city that I had never heard of. I would transit for several hours in China, then continue to Nepal. I booked the flight and prayed that it would be ok. I didn't have any other option.

The flights were fine. I met some other travellers, and we hung out together at the airport in China. I have found that most other travellers heading to and from Nepal are extremely friendly. I always enjoy hearing about their experiences and why they love Nepal as I do. But there was one more challenge to come. When coming through security, the staff requested me to remove my iPad from the backpack. As I am unused to doing this, I left it on the bench and did not pick it up with my other belongings. I walked several queues away and stood talking to my new travelling buddies for a few minutes. Suddenly, I sensed that I was missing something—the iPad. I ran back to the queue where I had been around 10 minutes before. There was the purple cover of my iPad, still sitting on the bench. No-one had taken it or moved it. All my notes for the conferences were contained on that iPad.

Thank you, Lord, I prayed. *Now, please, can I just get to Nepal!*

I arrived in Kathmandu within two hours of Carole's arrival. I raced back to the airport through the darkened streets in Lama's taxi. Waiting with hundreds of Nepali families also eagerly awaiting their loved ones' return home for festival time. Finally, Carole arrived, and we were reunited; both so happy to be there. When I awoke the next morning, I sat out on the little porch of my room at Tings Tea Lounge Hotel, with such a sense of peace. *I am exactly where I need to be, and in the right time to be here*, I thought. And I was.

For over 3 years, I had been hoping to deliver women's conferences in Nepal. It was finally happening. We had received financial donations from generous Australians so we could provide the conferences free of charge for the women. We also met with the women and staff at Vision Rehabilitation Centre. Spending time encouraging and praying with them. Carole is a talented artist and delivered a painting workshop at the rehab one afternoon. Every day meant meeting a new and eager group of women; I was thrilled with all of it.

Plans and schedules often change in Nepal. I had become used to that. I also have had years of experience in public ministry in lots of different settings and contexts. So, when things changed with the conference program or our transport or accommodation, I was not too bothered and able to roll with it. I remember how annoyed I was just a couple of years earlier when the *banda* strike cancelled my drama classes without notice. I felt for Carole at times when things changed at the last minute. I also tend to know in my mind what I will be doing and have my own ideas. I am also used to travelling and ministering in Nepal as the only foreigner in the team, so I don't always share all the information as it can get confusing with language and culture, etc. I had to remind myself that I may not need to know all the details, but others may require a little more information than I do. Carole was always very gracious.

After completing a program in Kokana, the church community in a leprosy colony, and several others in the surrounding village areas of Kathmandu, we came to a beautiful courtyard in the city. Positioned among geraniums and roses in pots, behind large gates and a concrete driveway, stood a large house with attached side buildings. Here we would participate in a program for the elderly. The program, called 'Happy Old Age Home,' started that year by a small group of church members to provide socialisation, activities, and spiritual input for the elderly in the surrounding streets. After climbing up a very small set of stairs, we entered a pleasant room full of brightly dressed men and women. They were all squeezed into a tiny room, covering every bit of floor space. Carole and I picked our way through the feet, handbags, Bibles, and scarves and found our chairs lined up against the wall.

Although I am always offered a chair, I often choose to sit on the floor. I love being near the women who I am going to minister with. Both Carole and I had the opportunity to speak and Romila, Ashok's wife, translated for us. As is my practice, at the end of our program, I offered to pray for everyone in the meeting. No-one ever seems to refuse. It takes a lot of time; but it is one of the most humbling and touching experiences. I am not anyone special, but when I hold their hand or touch their shoulder, and we seek the blessing and comfort of Jesus, beautiful things happen.

After about 45 minutes, we were nearing the back of the room after praying individually with around 50 people. Along the back wall stood a day bed of some sort. The most elderly and frail women sat and lay there. As I approached one partic- ular woman lying on her side, I sat down beside her and held her face. She looked into my eyes and smiled with love and hope. Together we began to weep as I declared God's goodness, mercy and strength over her life. We worshipped together, us two women; her in her faded red sari, wrinkled and sunken face, gnarled hands and raspy voice, but full with years of stories and faith. I stroked her face and kissed her forehead. Pressing my cheek against hers. She is one of millions of women across Nepal – but I will always remember her. These are the moments when you know that you are where you should be.

The two weeks came to an end. Carole and I parted, as she had some other friends to catch up with before she flew home. I also had other things to do and people to see. I was racing around to fit it all in. I even stayed up until 1am to go to my first Nepali cinema with a group of friends from the Pashmina and Knife shop. It was so much fun seeing their excitement as, surprisingly, it was also their first time at the cinema. I love how I still get surprised in Nepal. We walked home after the film in the early hours of the morning. The streets were dead, and even the dogs were still as we stepped over their curled bodies in the gutters. Dancing and laughing our way back towards Lazimpat. We eventually gave up walking and, finding a lone taxi, squeezed in and bumped our way home.

For my final two nights, I booked back into Tings Tea Lounge Hotel. It was my fifth stay there and was perfectly located just across the alleyway from Four Red Doors. Here I could enjoy a beautiful garden, and fresh food right in the heart of busy Lazimpat. Tings operated out of an older Nepali home, complete with ensuites and balconies. Each room had its own theme and décor. The staff had been there for years. Gita would turn up in the mornings just as I ordered breakfast, with her soft eyes and gentle *"Namaste, didi."* Dorje took care of reception and bookings. I always felt at home when staying there. It may have only been 3 stars in the guide books, but for me, it was perfect. After a breakfast of freshly baked bread, fruit salad, poached eggs and coffee, I was ready to enjoy my last day in Kathmandu.

I visited Christine (my German friend) and her children. She had moved out of Lazimpat and now rented a new home further away. It seemed a bit quieter without her close by. My favourite café for breakfast and lunch, owned by Jade, was shut. She closed it a few months earlier. Things had begun to feel different. It was my twelfth time in Nepal over a period of 7 years; I sensed that something was changing. I walked down the alley. The same alley I had walked down when I first visited Nepal alone, met Christine, found Four Red Doors, and settled into the area. The same alley that Pierre had gone to get *dudh* (milk) from the little corner shop and confused the shopkeeper with his pronunciation.

The same alley where Liz lost Darren, because he sat inside the barbershop for 1.5 hours instead of just dropping off the laundry. The same alley that my three grandsons ran down to meet Lama in his taxi, and where the fruit seller pushed his bicycle heavy with bananas and pomegranates. And where the puddles gather water, then mud and dust. Where children, in their crisp uniforms and plaited hair in ribbons, dodge the puddles as they walk to school. I can see it now in my mind. I can feel the cool morning air of Kathmandu and the quiet namaste of people passing me.

But on that day, I asked God, "Is there a new season?"

I didn't welcome it, but I couldn't stop it either.

I had fallen headlong in love with Nepal and its people. It was the surprise of my life. I never expected it. I didn't want it to end. I left Nepal in early October of 2019. Arriving home in time to meet my new grandson, Andy – bringing joy and love from heaven.

I had no timeframe for my return to Nepal.

I didn't know it would be so long.

Epilogue

As each new day begins, I feel the space between me and Nepal widening. It has been over a year since I hugged Lama goodbye and received my *Khada* scarf from him and his wife, Gita. Waving madly as I negotiated trolleys, Nepali families farewelling their sons off to labour in foreign nations, joining the queue to pass through security into Tribhuvan International Airport. The world has been concerned with other things since then.

But the yaks are still roaming the hillsides of the great Himalayas. Millions drink sweet milky tea every morning, sitting on doorsteps, and huddled around kerosene stoves chatting while rice and lentils cook. The children wander in and out, their dark shiny hair framing brown-eyed faces, and chickens scratch in the dust near the doorways. The traffic in Kathmandu, less, the horns quiet, as the country comes to grips with no international tourism. The roller doors stay down in Thamel, and the hotels have closed. Tings Tea Lounge and others closed for good. My friends message me.

"When you come Nepal?"

I don't know when I will return. International borders remain mostly closed as I write this.

However, WWP has continued to develop during this season. Although I have not been able to visit my beloved Nepal, God has been working through WWP and our partnerships. Despite all the global stresses and changes, as He always has. WWP began 4 years before with an idea to help Nepali women. Our mission: speak, defend, and invest. This year in partnership with local Nepali churches, we have leased land, dug a well, built a small home, sowed and harvested rice fields, supported a mother and baby, paid salaries for recovery staff at a rehab centre, provided emergency food relief for multiple families during strict lockdowns, invested in a tailoring business, and partnered with a new coffee shop.

The world may appear to have stopped for a pandemic, but the cries of those needs and concerns have not stopped reaching the ears of a loving and caring God. I am honoured to be able to be a part of meeting those needs.

When I look back at the doors, paths and steps that led me to where I am, I see the fingerprints of God everywhere. He inspired in me a love for other cultures and places when He revealed Himself to me as a 14-year-old. He joined Danny and me together in marriage through our family connections. He had a plan way back in 1982 when He sent Danny to Nepal with his family. He dragged me to Nepal in 2012 and ensured that I met the right people to stir my heart for that land. He whispers to me when I hike along trails, and when I'm quiet;

looking toward the mountains surrounding my home. He speaks to me about more plans and dreams.

Will I return to Nepal?

Yes, the season seems to have changed. Gone are some of the places I used to hang out: Jade's café, Tings Hotel. All my expat friends have left Nepal: Christine, Tim and others, returned to their own countries or settling elsewhere. What does the future hold for me and for Nepal?

It is eight years since Danny first took me to Nepal. I didn't even want to go. It took an act of God to get me there in the first place, and it may take another divine intervention for me to return. I remember the words that God spoke to me years before:

"My doors are automatic doors; they open as you approach them."

And I will keep approaching doors to see what lies ahead.

As I write this final chapter, I am reminded of the story of Jesus and the woman with her perfume. Breaking cultural taboos of the day and stepping into the room surrounded by important men, she breaks the jar of perfume, pouring the fragrance over His feet and hair. When the religious people around him grumbled about it, Jesus scolded them.

"She did what she could," He explained.

Am I willing, like that woman, to give out of my full, but imperfect life and pour myself and what I have over others? However that looks? Will it be said of me that *she did what she could?*

I hope so.

...From everyone to whom much has been given, so much more will be required; and to whom they entrusted much, of them (she), they will ask all the more.

(Luke 12:48b)

*For the latest news about Wise Woman
Project or to contact Sarah visit
www.wisewomanproject.com*

Clockwise from top left: Porters on the Annapurna Circuit Trek 1982, from Danny's photo album; Danny and Sarah's first visit to Nepal Oct/Nov (2012); Sarah at Lukla airport- known as one of the most dangerous in the world (2012).

our porters on our trek
left: Dukla right: Buddhaman.

This page top: Woman outside temple. This photo used as imagery for WWP (2013); *Below:* Approaching Gokyo village 4790m, sacred Lake No.3. (October 2013).

Opposite page top: Meeting our guide, Saimon in Lukla (2012); *Bottom:* Saimon in Didi's Teahouse, Lukla (2012).

This page from top: Daniel and Breanna at Namche Bazar (January 2016); Danny and Sarah at Annapurna Base Camp (2014); Women in Namche Bazar – photo used for a WWP poster (2016); *Opposite page:* Yaks around Namche Bazar (2016).

Clockwise from top left: Thar/goat around Namche Bazar (2016); Sarah handing over funds in Pramisa and Keshav's shop, Thamel Kathmandu (2016); Drama class with Gopi and Sarah in front row, Kathmandu (2016); Sarah on rooftop at the Dolphin Guesthouse (October 2016).

Clockwise from top left: Trekking Group at Phak Ding, second day of trek (2017); Shon, Parasu, Ashok and Sarah at the Girls Rehab centre in Kathmandu (2017); Jacob and a yak, near Kumjung, Sagarmatha National Park (2017); Ready to teach English at local school in Sotang, Solukhumbu (2017).

This page left: Nisha teaching Sarah how to cook Nepali food (2018); *Below:* Minu, Romila and Sarah during a Health and Hygiene Seminar, Chitwan (2018); *Opposite page top:* Darren, Sarah and Cathy on way back down from Gokyo Trek (2017); *Below:* Trekkers lined up at checkpoints in Everest Trekking Region during a busy season (October 2018)

Clockwise from top left:
From left – Debbie, Jess and Pierre in a teahouse while on Gokyo trek (2018); Sarah finally on top of Gokyo Ri, 5357m (2018); View from Gokyo Ri – Everest, Lotse, Makalu and Cho Oyu (2018); Porters and guides. From left, Rum, Prabesh, Pesal, Bikkash, Saimon at Dole (2018).

Clockwise from top left: On Lama's rooftop – *from back left:* Lama, Jessica, Adrian, Praasim, Danny, Sarah, Gita. Back row from right: Prahnaai, Beau, Joseph, Jacob (2019); Jessica and the yaks near Everest View Hotel, 3880m (2019); Trekking Group at Phak Ding on second day of trek (January 2019).

Top: In Sudarsan Khanal's Pashmina Shop, Thamel, Kathmandu
Clockwise from left: Joseph, Beau, Jacob, Khanal, Buni (2019);
Below: Sarah at Happy Old Age Home, Kathmandu (2019).